Mr and Mrs Mahon and Dan

When God Makes a Missionary

The Life Story of Edgar Mahon

W.F.P Burton

Edited by Anton Bosch

When God Makes a Missionary
The Life Story of Edgar Mahon

All rights and permission to revise and reprint "When God Makes a Missionary" granted to the Mahon Mission (now Zema) by the author, Wm. F. P. Burton, 27 June, 1959. Further permission to revise and reprint granted by Zema to Anton Bosch 20 June, 2016.

Copyright © 2017 Anton Bosch

All rights reserved. *No part of this book may be reproduced, stored in a retrieval system, or transmitted in any form by any means, whether electronic, mechanical, photocopying, audio recording, or otherwise without permission of the publisher.*

Disclaimer: *The Author and Publisher have applied their best efforts to make this book, including all footnotes and quotes, as accurate as possible. In the event that there may be any inaccuracy, this is unintentional and we apologize for such oversight.*

ISBN-13: 978-1976540905
ISBN-10: 1976540909

Published by: *Eldad Press,*
9070 Sunland Blvd, Sun Valley, CA, 91352 USA. anton@ifcb.net

Cover: *Mr and Mrs Mahon. Photo from the 2nd edition*

Editions:
1st – 1936
2nd – 1961
3rd – 2017

Contents

Maps 14

1   In the Whirl of the Gold Rush 17

2. Commissioned for Christ 23

3. The Salvation Banner Among the Mashona 27

4. Calamities That Brought Blessing 37

5. A Test of Faith and God's Provision 43

6. Blessings at Harrismith 49

7. Churches Organised 57

8. Five Years at Kalkoenkrantz 61

9. Headquarters at Mooigelegen 67

10. The Testimony Spreads in Natal 77

11. The Power of Song 83

12. The Gospel Spreads to Basutoland 87

13. At the Lichtenburg Diamond Diggings 99

14. Germiston Assembly 107

15. Startling Reactions 111

16. His Last Earthly Camp Meeting 117

Preface to the Third Edition

Two of the greatest influences in my life were Br "Willie" Burton and my great-grandfather, Edgar Mahon. I never had the privilege to meet Edgar Mahon as he passed away 16 years before I was born but I did learn about him through this book, oral traditions in our family, and the values he had passed on to his descendants.

As a young boy, I sat under the ministry of Br Burton and his passion for the Gospel had a profound and lasting impact on my life. The first sermon I can remember, of the many I heard as a boy, was one preached by Br Burton. One of my most prized possessions is an original copy of this book, previously owned by my grandmother, and daughter of Edgar Mahon – Evaline Gschwend (see p87).

Because of the profound impact both these men had on my own life and ministry, I wanted to perpetuate the availability of this book, to as many as possible, in the hope that they too may be inspired to serve the Lord and His church with the same dedication and zeal as these men.

The book was originally written by Br Burton and published in London in 1936.

In 1961, it was revised and reprinted by Alfred J and Margaret Mahon. They modernized the language, and moved a few of the stories around. They had added some additional material and deleted other parts.

My methodology in editing the book was to provide a fuller text, including all of Br Burton's original material, as well as most of the additional material added by Alfred and Margaret. In addition I also added several footnotes to explain uniquely South African words to a broader audience as well as converting monetary values to 2017 (USA) values.

The photographs are copies of the plates in the first edition – hence the bad quality. I decided to abandon most of the more modern (*circa* 1960) photographs from the second edition but did retain the photograph of Mr and Mrs Mahon from the second edition on the front cover.

My sincere thanks to my wife, Ina for capturing the original texts; Johan Potgieter for copy editing; my daughter, Beatrice Bosch for design advice; and my younger daughter, Evelyn Olsen, for designing the maps.

May this book inspire, bless, and encourage you, as it has me.

Anton Bosch
Los Angeles
July, 2017

Preface to Second Edition

Behind every movement, we look for a man. Today's great missionary movements were, in each case, started by a man, usually a man – highly individualistic, with a peculiar vision, and a dedicated drive in his ministry. Such was the man Edgar Mahon, whose heart God touched in South Africa to start a movement within the great missionary activities of that area of Africa.

Edgar Mahon was a true pioneer, and when we speak of "pioneer" we are not thinking so much geographically as we are in content of message and method. This invariably brings not the problem of penetrating a new culture, but the breaking with existing patterns of belief, or practices, and attitudes of those in the area already engaged in religious work.

In the beginning it was quite evident that Edgar Mahon did not conceive of himself as the founder of a mission, but rather he thought of himself as a man who had to go and tell people about the burden on his heart and bring them healing both of heart and body with the full message he had received from the Lord. This movement developed into a mission even though he never intended to found churches, but the logical, Biblical consequence of such work immediately produces regenerated Christians who in turn, sooner or later, will insist on being bound together into assemblies or fellowships, and thus churches resulted from this movement.

My own contacts with this mission, founded now many years ago by Edgar Mahon, had indicated that the mission has kept the message and the emphasis. It is a Gospel missionary agency that had as its goal to meet all of the needs of those who came seeking the Lord in their spiritual life and also in the physical and mental life. This is the Gospel at its best, and we are pleased that the mission is reprinting the biography of this man of God.

Clyde W. Taylor
Executive Secretary
Evangelical Foreign Missions Association

Preface to First Edition

A man's works tell more of what he is than a book can even hope to record. "Let us not talk about him," you say, "for at any time talk may be misleading. Let us see what he has accomplished." Elder Mahon's mission needs no advertising. Throughout South Africa, he and his beloved wife have left an epistle written not with ink, but in the hearts of many thousands; a letter read by natives and whites alike. He would be a rash man indeed who would try to assail their character or work. Government officials, native chiefs and headmen, miners, farmers, storekeepers, and unnumbered black saints to whom they have brought the gospel light, would rise to defend their name. Despite their quiet unassuming dispositions, they are among the best-known and best-loved people in the colony.

Since, then, there is no need either to advertise their work or to defend their characters, why do we write?

a. We do it under the conviction that God has directed us to tell the story.

b. We feel that this record of God's saving, healing, guiding and providing will encourage the faith of all who read it, leading others into similar ventures of self-abandonment for Christ and the lost.

c. Such a narrative, true in every detail, cannot but bring glory to our beloved Lord, Jesus Christ. It displays His faithfulness and power, showing that though nineteen centuries have passed the Acts of the Apostles is still an unfinished record, and that Jesus Christ is the same yesterday, today and forever.

We are not writing the story of a mission, though much of the activity of a whole mission must come under review. Our hearts reach out to tell many glorious stories of God's great power in other incidents, through other channels. The precious workers, native and white, will not feel neglected that we have largely confined our story to our dear old brother in Christ, Mr Edgar Mahon, and to the principles that he has laid down. Far be it from us to make light of the blessed part played by each member of the mission. God will not forget it, even though our space is too limited to record it.

For four years we have felt the urge to write this book. At last the opportunity came, and we spent a happy time in the home of the mission, heard the story from Mr Mahon's own lips, sat quietly with his children and the other workers, and asked from friends and neighbours their impressions of the testimony.

It was as though our heavenly Father permitted His aged witness to linger on until the precious record was put down, but even before the typing of the manuscripts was complete, the newspapers told of the Home-call of "One who had done more than any other man to introduce Christ to blacks and whites alike."

Comparisons are unwise. Many have done glorious work in evangelising South Africa, but at least the following pages will tell how much Christ, who is God, can do with one whose life is fully yielded to His blessed will.

W.F.P.B.

13

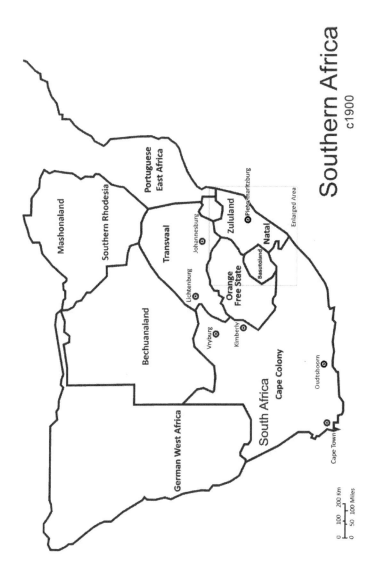

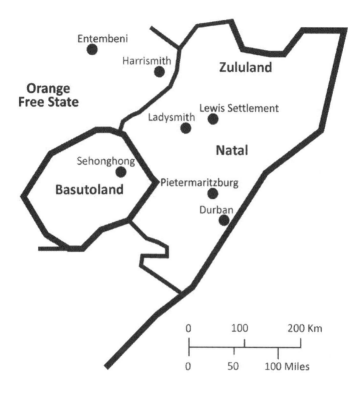

Chapter 1

In the Whirl of the Gold Rush

Life was very uneventful and quiet in the pastoral communities of South Africa's vast uplands, during the middle decades of the nineteenth century. Land was plentiful, grazing was good and populations were small. The people lived the simple life, and had very few wants. The country was far from the main streams of civilisation, and the tranquil minds of the farmers were little disturbed by what went on in the vast outside world.

Then a sudden change came over the country. First diamonds were found at Kimberley, and later gold was discovered on the Witwatersrand[1]. The locating of this unexplored wealth drew to those centres the most adventurous spirits of the globe.

A prospector, in taking a Sunday afternoon stroll across the grasslands, struck his foot against a rock that was unfamiliar to him. In idle curiosity he ground a piece upon a ploughshare, with a rusty bolt, and tried out the sample in a farmer's wife's frying pan. To his amazement he found that it was rich in gold. This started one of the most romantic

---

[1] The area around Johannesburg – now known as "Gauteng".

rushes in history. Thousands flocked to the "Rand"[2]. There were no railways and the roads were only rough tracks. Ox and mule-wagons were the usual means of transport, and during the years 1886-1887 a wonderful new city sprang up where before there had been nothing but bare "veld"[3]. Within half a century Johannesburg was to be a city of little less than a million inhabitants.

Among those who flocked to the mines was a Mr Alfred Mahon, who had made his living at trading and transport riding. He had a family of six sons and three daughters. Of Irish parentage, they had lived in Mafeking, and the father of the family was well known among the natives as their friend.

In 1886 we find some of the family trekking from Kimberley, to set up a bottle-store[4] among the miners of the newly-discovered gold reef. Soon after the Mahons moved to Johannesburg, the Salvation Army commenced operations there. Two ladies, Captain Merrit and Lieutenant Watkinson, were the first officers. They believed in music but at first they were without the necessary musicians. However, in the absence of a complete band, they made a start with the drum, much to the scorn of the older people, and the delight of the children.

Hecklers were many and sympathies were few. Those brave pioneers suffered abundant reproach for the name of the Lord Jesus. Reckless daredevils were everywhere. The wildest elements of five continents could be found among the crowds to whom the intrepid ladies preached. Indeed it was in the hearts of just such men as these that the all-conquering power of the gospel won its most glorious trophies.

---

[2] Short for "Witwatersrand".

[3] South African for grassland or prairie.

[4] Liquor store.

One day little Charles Mahon was attracted by the thumping of the Army drum, and followed the crowd to the meeting place. He was used to the wild life of pioneer days, but here was something quite fresh to him. "Blood and Fire" was the motto that floated from the Army flagpole, but this was not the all-too-prevalent brawling, fighting and arson. Their message told him of One who had shed His precious blood as a propitiation for the sins of a guilty world, and of a risen Christ who could transform the vilest and most abandoned lives into the image of God, who could pour out upon His children a baptism in the Holy Ghost and fire which would send them forth aflame to win a lost and perishing humanity.

Little Charlie Mahon was attracted, but that was all. He was enjoying his life of sin, and not at all ready to change it for purity and holiness. One thing puzzled him however. He could not keep away from the Army meetings. At first it was the drum which called him, but now he was held by a power he could not explain. Again and again he found himself drawn with cords of love, and wooed by the winsome pleading of the gospel message, until he became a regular attendant at the services, and the Salvation Army hall fell under his parents' suspicion. What were they doing to the boy? Why was he constantly found following in the wake of the drum?

In those days there was plenty of other excitement on the Rand: sprees and brawls where jugglers and mountebanks[5] earned a precarious living at the expense of the gold-diggers. What was it that attracted the lad to those two women in strange bonnets? Charlie's parents determined to follow him.

A certain Divisional Staff-Captain, Pasco, was giving his testimony when they entered. Every word seemed like an arrow forged on God's anvil and specially directed at their

---

[5] Swindler, charlatan, confidence trickster.

own hearts. Their bottle-store was damning the very souls that these brave ladies were struggling to save. At the end of Captain Pasco's address, he made a stirring appeal, but there was another power other than man's in that entreaty. God's Holy Spirit was behind it. Soon, to Charlie's amazement, he saw his own parents going forward to the penitent form and seeking salvation. The last scrap of his opposition broke down, and he too went weeping to the front, found salvation through faith in the Lord Jesus Christ, and left that hall with the great assurance in his heart that he was at peace with God. After that things moved quickly in the Mahon family. Soon four other sons were saved, as well as older members of the family.

At that time Charlie's elder brother, Edgar, was anxious to join them in Johannesburg, and with that in view, he offered his services to a transport rider, who was taking three wagon-loads of whisky to the mines. They had not gone far on the journey when the leader of the group of wagons put young Edgar up to his way of helping himself to the whisky, which was in his barrels. He knocked up the top band of a barrel, pierced the staves with a bradawl, had a native blow through the hole thus made, and then caught the spirit as it oozed out. The hole was then stopped with a splinter of wood, the band was knocked back into place on the barrel, and nobody could tell that the contents had been tampered with. Soon they overtook other similar wagons, also conveying spirits to the mines, and the whole journey was one long drunken brawl.

Arriving in Johannesburg, Edgar met one of his uncles, and, not knowing of the great changes that had taken place, he offered him some whisky. The uncle replied, "No, Edgar! I have finished with whisky once and for all, and with tobacco too, for I have been converted to God." That remark puzzled and convicted Edgar. He found that his younger brother Charlie was on fire for God, that his parents were saved, and that the bottle-store was abandoned. Thus, he too went to the Salvation Army and yielded himself to the Lord Jesus Christ.

What an amazing revolution had taken place in the family! God's power had so changed them that five of the six sons now commenced to learn brass instruments and to take their place in the Army band – the first Army band in Fordsburg. Day after day saw them, as soon as their work was over, marching around the streets of Johannesburg, preaching the gospel, helping the friendless and fallen, and seeing "drunks", "stiffs" and "criminals" made "new creatures in Christ Jesus"[6].

Edgar Mahon soon built up a fine transport and agency work, so that, had he allowed the moneymaking craze to grip him, he might have become a wealthy man. His mind was set on more enduring treasure, however, and it was a splendid sight when those six brothers took their stand each evening in the thick of the rough mining crowds, playing, singing and witnessing for the Lord Jesus.

Had the rowdy element been unhindered, it would have been impossible to continue the open-air meetings, for often, – rotten eggs, decayed vegetables, brandy and other things were thrown at the noble little group that dared to raise its standard against sin. There were men in Johannesburg at that time, who would have cut a man's throat if they thought they could get half-a-crown[7] from him. Always, however, there were some in the crowd whose sympathies were sufficiently strong to take the part of the Salvationists.

---

[6] Thirty-eight years later, Charlie Mahon is bandmaster of Benoni S.A. band. Thank God for a gospel that not only saves men, but keeps them. One day a remark was made to the writer "I've got no time for much so-called Christianity, but there's a fellow called Charlie Mahon, who works on our mine, and I can only say that if that's the genuine brand of Christianity, then I want it, for he *lives* what he preaches."

[7] 25 cents equivalent to $11(US) in 2017.

It was the rule of the Mahons that when any mischief seemed to be brewing they would put the women in the centre of the ring, and make a protecting barrier about them. Thus, these fine, stalwart young men, who could have thrashed many of the assailants who molested the meetings, learned to stand quietly under the Devil's artillery, giving love for hatred, and graciousness for brutality. Spattered and befouled by the filth that would otherwise have struck their beloved officers, these Mahons refused to allow thoughts of resentment to enter their hearts, but prayed as their Master before them: "Father, have mercy on their souls. Save them. They are not attacking us. They are fighting against Thee. Oh save them and make them Thine own."

Eternity alone will reveal all those who owe their salvation to the dignity and patience of these young converts when under fire. Their lives and their demeanour were witnessing even when their words were drowned by scoffs and jeers.

Chapter 2

Commissioned for Christ

Steadily and persistently a conflict began to grow in the heart of Edgar Mahon. He could often make twenty or thirty pounds a day[8]. The simple, back-veld farmers had little idea of the value of money, and when they brought their wagonloads of produce into the mining area, they were fleeced and swindled shamelessly. The farmers realised that they must have someone of principle and integrity who could act as their agent, and singled out Edgar for the work.

At the same time a still, small voice kept calling him to a more important task. It meant a lot for this high-spirited, able, young man to abandon every visible means of support, and to launch out into a life of faith. The Lord Jesus won the battle, and Edgar entered Beaconsfield Training Institute near Kimberley, under Staff-Captain Smith.

This officer was a rigid disciplinarian, but all his student officers loved him, and thanked God for the opportunity to train under him. In accordance with Army regulations, Edgar had to promise that he would not marry for three years. It happened, however, that while he was undergoing his six months' training, that a certain Miss Joey Buchler

---

[8] $2,800 and $4,130 in 2017.

attended the meetings, and though he had never even had the opportunity to exchange a word with her, his whole heart went out in longing for the girl. Had his secret become known by word or act, his days at the training institute would have been cut short. When however, his term of training ended, he felt it time to make some move toward making his intentions known. By this time Miss Buchler herself had entered the training institute for women officers.

Edgar decided to unburden his heart to Staff-Captain Smith. He received very sympathetic treatment, and God worked in a beautiful way to permit him to become better acquainted with his future wife's parents. It was thus: From the training home, Edgar Mahon was given command of the corps at Vryburg, a small town between Kimberley and Mafeking. He enjoyed his work immensely, but longed for an opportunity to reach the natives.

He was suddenly laid low by a dose of dysentery and was hurried to the hospital at Kimberley. Mrs Buchler, Joey's mother, an excellent certified nurse, was a big-hearted Christian woman who delighted to have young Christians in her home. When they were sick, she loved to care for them until strength returned. She heard of young Mahon's condition, and asked that he might be allowed to recuperate in her home.

Captain Mahon (as he was then) confided in her the longings of his heart, and it was arranged that Miss Buchler should visit her home for a week-end, that he might have the opportunity of conversing with her personally. The young lady had never spoken to him before. Moreover, she had devoted herself wholeheartedly to God's service, and was content to remain as she was, if only God's work might have all her energies. Thus, poor Edgar did not receive an affirmative answer. At least he was encouraged however, that she did not refuse him point-blank. They agreed to correspond, and so parted.

As strength returned, the young captain received notice that he was to be one of a party to go northward to Fort Salisbury, in an effort to evangelise both the whites and natives of Mashonaland.

Chapter 3

Planting the Salvation Banner among the Mashona

In May, 1891, Captain Mahon was one of five picked men sent to commence a gospel testimony in and around Fort Salisbury[9] in Rhodesia.

The journey from Kimberley took about six and a half months. Unusually late rains made the first seven weeks one long nightmare. The party took a huge covered wagon with eighteen splendid oxen and three horses. It was impossible for them to carry sufficient provisions for such a long trip. They simply had to live by what they could shoot. At times the roads were so bad that these pioneers had to off-load the wagon six to eight times a day. It was winter, and they would spend the greater part of a night up to their knees in water, digging the wagon wheels out of mud holes. When at last better weather set in, these tough pioneers had to contend with wild beasts, dysentery, malaria and tsetse flies.

In passing through dry areas, they felt the lack of water keenly. When they did find water, it was at times the foulest and most stagnant stuff. More than once they were lost. Even the natives who were with them wept and lost heart. Jackals and wild dogs hung about the caravan. (In their journals the

---

[9] Later named "Salisbury" – present day Harare in Zimbabwe.

Salvationists called these formidable beasts wolves.) Lions treed their native helpers. Once, only a good shot at a wild partridge averted starvation in the wilderness.

The sparsely inhabited country through which they travelled was so new to white men that the natives believed these newcomers had arrived to rob them.

Imagine them struggling through wide, shallow streams, where deep sand impeded their wagon wheels. Then, see them toiling up rocky hills, the horsemen riding ahead to find a route up which the wagons could follow. Eleven of the oxen died and two were carried off by hyenas. Once Captain Mahon lay for two days, lost in the wilds and so sick with fever that he could not stir to find his way back to the wagon.

The fare of these Salvationists consisted of such mixed menus as zebra, wild pig and giraffe. So great were the hardships that many a strong man would have lost heart. It was only the assurance of God's guidance that kept them steadfastly facing forward and plunging farther and farther into the unknown. At last they reached Mashonaland, and set to work among the 400 whites in Fort Salisbury, as well as the thousands of natives in the surrounding area.

The administrative officers of the Government encouraged them and gave them two stands on which to build. They erected a hall to seat 100 as well as buildings for themselves and for the divisional commander. They did all the work themselves – cutting stone, making brick, and even going into the wilds to cut poles for the roofs. They also started a big farm, employing 500 natives. Their record accounts of long, sleepless nights spent in pleading for souls, stories of gospel marches around Fort Salisbury, and of sitting beside the sick, nursing them back from the illness of fever.

When funds were low, a tea meeting produced twenty-five pounds. It must be realised, however, that European commodities were extremely dear: a bag of meal cost ten pounds[10], a tin of condensed milk ten shillings[11], a single candle six shillings and sixpence[12], and a pound (500g) tin of jam thirteen shillings and sixpence[13].

Superhuman obstacles lay in their paths. Not only was the language difficult, but the natives were degraded and superstitious. The white people were unstable. Of fifteen who professed conversion one week, only four stood true to their profession on the week following.

Bloodshed was nothing uncommon. Chief Lobengula, of the Matabele, would send his armies to raid the Mashona, killing the grown men and carrying away the wives and oxen. Consequently, the natives lived in almost inaccessible spots among the hills. Once these Mashona killed a white man. For reprisal, the whites of Fort Salisbury burned down four native villages, killing and wounding men, women and even children.

When tsetse flies killed the horses, Mahon and his companions had to use donkeys. The hyenas however, would often seize these for prey. At one time when the missionaries were following some donkeys that had been stampeded by hyenas, they came face-to-face with four lions, and were obliged to return without their animals.

Eventually disease so ravaged the settlement that fully half the white people either died or left the country. Those who stayed were like skeletons and there were hardly sufficient strong ones to nurse the sick. In their extremity, the whites turned to the consolation of religion, and eagerly devoured every page of the *War Cry*[14] as it was distributed among

---

[10] $1,076.

[11] $54.

[12] $35.

[13] $73.

[14] *The War Cry* is the Salvation Army's magazine. It is now in its 137th year of publication.

them. At last Captain Mahon, among others, was ordered by the doctor to leave at once. He had, had a long period of weakness and fevers, and it was felt that any further stay in the country would mean his death.

His letters show how ready he was to stay and die among the Mashona, should necessity demand it. His *all* was upon the altar, but God had other work for him. Some of his companions died, and one was killed in the Mazoe Valley Revolt. Though the enterprise started so unpropitiously, it was not abandoned. The work still continued, and the precious souls saved during those early days shine as bright jewels in the Saviour's crown. Even on his way back to civilisation, Mahon's affections continued to go out to those degraded and despoiled Mashona.

At this time we are allowed to follow the course of a very beautiful and growing love between Captain Mahon and Captain Buchler. Friendship was deepening into something more permanent. The two were getting to know and understand each other by correspondence. Every letter was filled with a desire for God's will alone and with a glorious abandonment to His guidance. Thus, we watch with delight how God was planning to unite those two lives for His glory. Each urged the other to live at full stretch for Jesus only, yet He who said, "It is not good for a man to be alone; I will make a help meet for him," was planning just the very help that would best fit into the life of His servant, Captain Mahon.

After his return from Mashonaland, Captain Mahon was appointed to Robertson, Georgetown[15], and Oudtshoorn in turn. It was while Captain Mahon was at Oudtshoorn that a happy wedding took place and Joey Buchler became his wife. How graciously God led in this matter. Who can estimate the blessing to a man of God when his Master gives

---

[15] Modern George.

him a helpmeet likeminded with himself, a woman who is a hundred percent for God?

His younger brother Charles came out of training about the same time, and the accounts of their early campaigns are thrilling.[16] It must be remembered that the Salvation Army was not the well-known and respected institution that we have today. It was a young and untried concern, steadily winning its way against the most violent opposition that the enemy of souls could raise. Charlie was imprisoned three times for open air preaching. Once, in Port Elizabeth, the townsfolk bailed him out, and twice he served his sentence. He was only about seventeen years of age, but he was

---

[16] Faith triumphed and brought souls to the Lord Jesus even during the most trying circumstances. Charles Mahon rode one day for hours through a blinding swarm of locusts near his birthplace, Thabanchu. He had to tie up his sleeves and trousers, and put a handkerchief over his head, and then, putting his face down, allowed his horse to drive through the swirling billions of ravenous insects. The veld was bare. Every blade of grass nibbled off.

Later he arrived at the home of a poor family. They thought by his Salvation Army uniform that he was a policeman. However, he reassured them and commenced to talk with them. They had no thought for anything but that approaching swarm, however. "If those locusts reach my farm, I am a ruined man," declared the farmer. "All my month s of toiling will be eaten up in a few minutes."

The swarm was approaching in an ugly, ominous brown cloud. Charles took the whole family down to the borders of their little farm, and there he lifted his hands to God and cried for deliverance from the locusts. The power of the Spirit was upon him, and he does not know how long he continued in prayer, but on opening his eyes, there was not a locust in sight. Where they had gone that little group did not know, but at least they did not touch a blade of grass on the prayer-protected farm.

The old farmer and his wife professed faith in the Lord Jesus there and then, and were so amazed at the revelation of answered prayer that they begged Charles Mahon to stop with them.

determined to stand for the liberty of preaching, and today the freedom of gospel which South Africa enjoys, is largely due to the heroic efforts of these and similar young "undauntables for Jesus."

Oudtshoorn Town Council refused to give anyone the right to preach in the streets, and the only place in which the Army could witness, was on a private stand. Moreover, they had to be indoors by a certain hour, or fines would result. So eager were some to get the Army into any possible trouble that a policeman used to stand at the door of the Army Hall, watch in hand, hoping to catch them out after the appointed hour. He never succeeded however.

Captain Mahon approached the Mayor of Oudtshoorn, asking that he might have permission to preach where he would in the town. The Mayor was most curt, and declared, "The people don't want you, and I don't, either. No, you shall not have permission". "I beg your pardon, sir," replied Mahon, "but the people do want us, and I will make it my business to get them to sign a paper to that effect".

The Mayor now worked himself into a towering rage, stamping his foot and shouting, "Then I will also draw up a document with the signatures of the people, to the effect that they do not want you." Mahon went to work without delay, obtaining the signatures by turn of all the ministers of religion, all the canteen keepers, all the hotel keepers, and practically all the shop and storekeepers. He explained to them that since even circuses were permitted to parade through the town and to pitch where they would, surely preachers of the gospel should be accorded equal rights.

They saw the reasonableness of it, and stood behind the petition. At the next meeting of the Town Council, Mahon presented his petition. The Mayor was furious, for in all the town he had only been able to induce twenty-five people to sign his petition. He openly insulted his fellow-counsellors and the citizens who had put him into office, declaring that he "had no idea that there were so many fools in Oudtshoorn as this paper proved." All his raving and stamping was useless, however, and it was decided that for three nights each week the Army could march through the town with its band, and stand where it would to preach and testify. This privilege continued to the time of writing.

Another formidable difficulty faced the young captain: This was chiefly through the opposition of a blacksmith, a bullying, blustering fellow, who boasted that he had broken up every other meeting and would break up this one too. He disturbed, insulted, and refused to recognise the authority of the captain.

At last things came to a head when Mahon asked his congregation to stand for prayer. This, the blacksmith refused to do. He sat in his place and would not budge. Mahon would not continue the service until the blacksmith complied with his command. A deadlock lasted for some ten minutes, but eventually the blacksmith stood and moreover he did not refuse Mahon's commands again. After the meeting his chums made sport of him, and said, "You've met your match this time. At last there's somebody who will force you to obey". This so enraged the blacksmith, that he offered a sum of money to anyone who would upset the Salvation Army meetings.

The next Tuesday there was a private meeting for Salvationists, and as they knelt at prayer, a handful of lighted firecrackers was thrown in at the fanlight. It was a most dangerous trick, and Mahon prayed that God would enable him to bring the perpetrators to book.

He had a good idea of the rowdies of the town, and decided that a certain young boot repairer was the most obvious to have had part in the outrage. The next day he visited this bootmaker, and said, "My lad, this is a most serious affair.

There was paraffin[17] under the platform, and the weather being hot, the ladies present had dresses of light material which could easily have caught fire. This is a matter for the court-house and the prison." The young man was visibly moved at this. Mahon went on: "The only condition upon which I will not take the matter further is that you give me the names of all who are implicated in the outrage, and the part they played." On the next day, the young fellow came to Mahon in a thoroughly frightened mood, confessed all, gave the names of his accomplices and apologised humbly.

The other participants were now visited, without revealing how their names were known. They were told that unless they gave a written apology, which should be read out in public, they would have to face the police. The bullying blacksmith was terribly frightened. He would do anything to make amends. All the interrupters of the meetings signed an apology and from that time forward the work went ahead in peace and blessing. Numbers were added to the Lord Jesus, and the corps was built up.

From Oudtshoorn they were moved down to Natal[18], and at last Captain Mahon's aspirations were realised. He was put into native work, as an instructor in a training institute. He had only an elementary knowledge of the native languages, but as Mr and Mrs Mahon taught the black folk, they themselves learned more and more of both languages and customs.

A magnificent success followed their efforts, and as they moved from place to place, in white and native work, God used them in glorious revivals. At times there would be as many as two thousand natives in the open air services in Pietermaritzburg. Even better than coming to the meetings,

---

[17] Kerosene.
[18] The area on the east coast of South Africa, now known as KwaZulu-Natal.

very many came to the Cross, and were cleansed and made 'new creatures' in the precious blood of the Lord Jesus.

As a rule, the crowds that listened in the open air or indoors were so sympathetic that the Salvationists had little to do in keeping order. When occasional rowdies interrupted, it was the outsiders who took them by the scruff of the neck, manhandled them and threw them out.

On one occasion, however, two young men came night after night, insulting, making noises, and doing all in their power to hinder the meetings and ridicule the workers. Captain Mahon went to the police and asked the sergeant to come and stop them. The sergeant looked him up and down, and remarked, "You look as if you could do that job yourself. Why do you come to me?" Captain Mahon replied, "Do you realise that you are suggesting that we take the law into our own hands? If I did any such thing you would have to take action against me." The sergeant replied, "I know those young men and how they have goaded you on to desperation. You throw them out and I will see that no harm overtakes you for it."

In the next meeting they were even more rowdy than usual. They had brought some little noisy instrument into the meeting, and at intervals interrupted with weird sounds. After warning, and even standing by the culprits to try to induce them to desist, Captain Mahon made a feint at one, and catching him a "Full Nelson" on the neck, marched him helplessly out of the hall, to the shame of the culprit and the amusement of the crowd. Once outside, the interrupter was set down more emphatically than gently. His young lady came complaining to Mahon that he had hurt her sweetheart, but it was his own fault. From that day quietness and respect reigned in the meetings.

Chapter 4

Calamities that Brought Blessing

One cannot work as the Mahons were working without feeling the results in one's body. The crowds that came and found life and peace in the Lord Jesus knew little of the way the work was beginning to tell on the bodies of their beloved leaders.

It was while they were working among the Zulus in the Lewis Settlement[19] that Captain Mahon's health began to fail. His lungs had been affected while he was in Mashonaland and now the dreaded tuberculosis was killing him. He had been in the process of erecting a stone church when he became ill. He was coughing blood and often had to lie prostrate. At this time too, the Captain's only means of transportation was horseback, and frequently he would return home from visiting his flock at the point of collapse from weakness and loss of blood. The doctor who examined him told him that one lung was useless and the other badly affected, and that he could not expect to live for more than a month.

---

[19] Near present-day Helpmekaar, south of Dundee.

Meanwhile Mrs Mahon's stepbrother, Rev J U Buchler, was experiencing great blessings in God's power to save and heal. On hearing of their plight, he wrote to them not to give up hope. The Lord could heal them. He also sent them testimonies of people who had been healed. This led to new hope. At this time Rev Buchler had been invited to Pietermaritzburg to pray for a sick woman. He decided to attempt to visit his sister and brother-in-law. This was in 1897.

Travel in those days was difficult. The nearest railway from the Mahons was about forty miles away. It was during the rainy season and there were no bridges over the swollen rivers. After many adventures, however, he arrived safely. At the station, on the way, the daughter of a Zulu chief was sick. Buchler saw her plight and prayed for her. Later they heard that she was instantly healed, and went back to tell her people the good news that there was deliverance from sickness in Jesus' name.

Appalled at the condition of Captain Mahon, Rev Buchler taught them about divine healing, laid hands on the Captain in the name of the Lord Jesus, and God healed him. Health and strength were regained so speedily that a month later, instead of dying, Captain Mahon was able to continue with the building and to carry on his work.

At that time they had quite an extensive little pharmacy, for amelioration of suffering natives. When Buchler saw it he remarked, "Behold, O Israel, thy gods, the dispensary that led thee out of sickness." This struck a new chord in the hearts of the Salvationists. They determined to renounce medicines from that time forward. The very last bottle, one to which they clung pathetically, was supposedly a cure for snakebite. Even that had to go however, and they cast themselves entirely upon God.

The restoration to health and strength of their beloved leader brought immediate results. Crowds flocked to hear the Rev Buchler, bringing their sick. Even through the medium of interpretation, the people were swayed by the power of God when Rev Buchler stood up to preach. When the invitation was given for the sick and suffering to come forward for the laying on of hands, very many came, and were instantly healed. Among them was an aged chieftainess, of over ninety years. She had been ill for a long time but God healed her and she went rejoicing to tell her people that she was now strong and moreover, "had God inside."

In the Salvation Army, baptism was not practiced. Mrs Mahon had been baptised when she was a girl of fifteen. Baptism was discussed one day as they rode along with Rev Buchler. As they passed a pool, Captain Mahon said, "Here is water. What doth hinder me to be baptized?" They dismounted from their horses and a baptismal service was held, then and there.

The natives begged Buchler to stay with them and pray for them, but he said, "No. Captain Mahon is your minister. He can pray for you. You come to him for prayer." The natives came in crowds. So great was the press that they had to let a hundred into the church at a time, instruct them, pray for them, and then receive a hundred more. The results in salvation were glorious, for many of those who were healed found life and peace in the Lord Jesus Christ. Captain and Mrs Mahon even had to take their meals in the church because the people were flocking to hear the gospel and to be delivered of their sicknesses.

The crowds that flocked to Lewis Settlement for healing had come from far away, and in many cases had made no provision. The Mahons had nothing but their regular Salvation Army rations. There was just a small maize[20] patch and they supplemented their diet with fresh green mealies[21]. Mrs Mahon could not see those who had come to them

---

[20] Called "corn" in the US and "mealies" in South Africa.
[21] Corn on the cob.

remain hungry, so she would say to the native girl who helped them with the work, "Put on a pot of mealies." Another wagonload of people would arrive, and still another. Again the orders: "Put on a pot of mealies." Normally the mealie patch should soon have been used up, but it yielded more and more. Sometimes Mrs Mahon would apologise to her native guests, saying, "I'm sorry you have had so little". But the invariable reply was, "We have had more than enough to eat." Day after day the crowds increased, and nobody but God knows how it was done, and still the wee mealie patch held out. The God who provided for five thousand with five loaves and two little fishes was now working a similar miracle for His children at the Lewis Settlement.

All these stirrings were duly reported by the officers to their headquarters. They met with very little encouragement however, and were told that, since they were well, now they should return to Pietermaritzburg.

Still the people, black and white, came in crowds to hear. All the town was stirred, and the Salvationists stood with cornet and concertina, witnessing in the open air. From all round the district came pleas for further teaching. Mahon did what the great founder of the Army did before him, he endeavoured to continue his local work as well as to minister to those farther afield. This did not please those in authority.

Upon their return to Pietermaritzburg the Mahons found the corps in a lamentable condition. Many had backslidden. The cause was involved in a debt, and in order to extricate themselves, the previous officers had descended to such lengths of begging and money raising that they had brought the testimony into disrepute and shame. The Mahons decided that they would not take collections or make God's work cheap by begging from the unsaved. In answer to prayer the money was sent in from the least expected quarters and in a short time the work was in a flourishing condition financially and spiritually.

To the captain's surprise he received a peremptory letter, indicating that his step in being baptised was "against orders," that he was to desist from visiting outside Pietermaritzburg, unless by orders of his major, and that since the Army was only concerned with winning souls he was to stop 'this nonsense of praying for the sick.' It was a terrible blow. Here were hundreds coming to find not only healing for their bodies, but salvation for their souls. The Mahons knew well that they were in God's will, and working according to His plan, yet their superiors in the Army treated them as though they were in error. What were they to do? Streams of natives were coming on foot and in wagons seeking light and deliverance. They could not turn them away, so they determined to obey God rather than man, and continued their ministries to the suffering and lost.

At the next General Army Conference in Johannesburg, the editor of the *War Cry* rose and launched an attack on Mahon and his methods in most unchristian terms, speaking for about twenty minutes. Before he had finished there were about eight on their feet to answer him and to take Mahon's part. Captain Mahon himself sat quietly, not even lifting his voice to vindicate himself, but the other officers were thoroughly aroused. The Editor said, "We are here to raise the drunkard and the fallen, and not to pray for the sick." Someone called back, "When did our Lord repeal His orders to lay hands on the sick?" The whole meeting seemed thoroughly in favour of Mahon. The Divisional Commissioner endeavoured to restore order, but pandemonium reigned and eventually the meeting had to be closed.

Even while this Salvation Army meeting was in progress in Johannesburg, a native girl was brought in for prayer. She had not spoken for four months and could move nothing but her eyelids. Mrs Mahon and a native woman prayed with her, and then taking her by the arms told her to get up in Jesus' name and walk. Immediately she arose, walked and spoke. God had healed her on the spot. Yet in spite of such an outstanding miracle, the opponent of Mr Mahon remained unmoved in his objections to divine healing.

Mahon was pressed on all sides by sympathisers. Superior officers said, "Come to my field. We want you, and you shall pray for the sick to your heart's content if only you will win souls for Christ." He could see, however, that it would only be a temporary respite if he were welcomed into someone else's area. Sooner or later he would be moved and all the old difficulty would be restarted. He decided to resign. Those in high command begged him to stay on. They refused his resignation, and even promoted him to the title of "Ensign" to induce him to remain.

The whole question was revolved again and again in their minds and in prayer. As the greater revelation of God's will was unfolded to them, they could not be limited by remaining in a man-made system. They must be loyal to the whole Word of God, and thus they once more sent in their resignation, and a wire came back telling them to vacate their quarters in a week's time.

Chapter 5

A Test of Faith and God's Provision

Captain and Mrs Mahon had stood by their convictions, but now that the results faced them, they were perplexed. They had saved nothing, and now had four children. God had given them twin daughters while they were in Pietermaritzburg. Even as they packed their goods and put them out on the veranda[22], they did not know where to go. A Mr Lantz, near the Lewis Settlement, had often begged them to pay him a visit. They decided to spend a week or two there, that they might have time for quiet waiting on God. Mr Walter Puttrill, near Harrismith, told them that if they would come and settle on his farm to do evangelistic work, he would provide them with a house and such food as the farm afforded.

In Mr Lantz's home, one of the Mahon babies had a very bad attack of croup one night. Mrs Lantz said, "It sounds as if the little one is dying. They have renounced all medicine. Now we will see what they do!" The Mahons rose and dressed, and then committed their child into God's keeping. At once the coughing died down and the child was soon sleeping peacefully.

---

[22] Roofed area on the front of the house: stoop or porch.

Mr Mahon met an old friend whom he had known in Mashonaland and this man gave him a pound[23]. He got another five pounds for his bicycle, and at the last moment a letter came from an unknown person asking him to accept five pounds for his own personal needs. More-over God provided that all their luggage should be transported free of charge, though to this day they do not know how.

They arrived at Harrismith station with only one shilling and sixpence[24] in their pockets. Mr Puttrill had sent a wagon to bring them and their goods to his farm. The native wagon drivers said they had no food, so Mr Mahon gave them his last shilling and sixpence, and went forward into the unknown without a penny in his pocket.

It was not a promising outlook from man's viewpoint, but God was with them, and they were as well provided for as though they had thousands in the bank. Mr Puttrill was a tower of strength to the Mahons. He was of missionary parents and a devoted Christian. Mr and Mrs Mahon and their four children stayed on his farm for six months, witnessing to all around. These were times of quiet refreshing. In the evening they would set out, accompanied by native Christians, to preach in all the farm locations[25] around. As soon as the natives heard Mr Mahon's cornet they flocked to listen to the message of life. Many were converted to God and the whole neighbourhood was blessed and stirred.

Then the Anglo-Boer War broke out, and the English-speaking people began to leave the Orange Free State. At first, the Mahons thought of staying on and trusting them-selves to God's care, while keeping strictly neutral. Later however, the resident Magistrate told them that there was no

---

[23] $107.

[24] $8.

[25] Worker's compounds where each farm housed their workers.

such thing as neutrality and if they would not take sides with the Orange Free State, they must get out with all speed.

The few necessaries were packed up. Mr Puttrill put a wagon at their disposal and they set out eastward. The journey down the steepest part of the great Drakensberg Mountains, after dark, was a nerve-racking experience. Native drivers plunged on in the darkness over ant-heaps and ant bear holes, first one side of the wagon and then the other being up in the air. More than once the road was lost. The native drivers wanted to give up in despair. They were urged, however, to put their trust in God and to press forward, leaving the animals to choose the way. Mrs Mahon was indefatigable. She showed her simple trust by singing hymns and quoting texts so that the natives and children might be kept from fear.

Eventually, they reached Ladysmith, where they found Mr Mahon's mother, sisters and brothers, who had fled from Johannesburg. Together they hired a house, but were scarcely settled when they found themselves surrounded. Two days after their arrival in Ladysmith, it was besieged (2 November, 1899).

At first they didn't realise what a serious matter this war really was, but when the famous "Long Tom" cannon started to send shells all over the town carrying death and destruction where least expected, the people scrambled into pits and trenches, or hid in the river bed. The authorities discouraged this, for it was found that the people thus exposed themselves to enemy fire even more than if they remained in their houses. Hence, they simply settled down to take life as happily and philosophically as possible.

The town was under martial law. Nobody knew how long the siege was to last and the authorities forbade all Christian services.

At first Mrs Mahon made tea and ginger-beer to serve free to the troops. Later, they begged her to let them pay her and she sold it for a small fee. Christian soldiers soon found them out and came to visit. Because the badly cooked camp food caused dysentery and other sicknesses, the Mahons made them porridge. Later the soldiers persuaded them to make the porridge regularly so that they could purchase it. For six weeks they were served a three-penny[26] plate of porridge in the morning, and such things as a plate of soup or a cup of tea in the evening. Then the food supply came to an end. The authorities confiscated all stores, and food was rationed daily. Even the flesh of the horses that dropped dead in the streets was cut up and eaten.

The dead and wounded were constantly carried past their home. On a hill nearby was a cannon. Every time it was fired, the windows shook and the babies became nervous and ill. For a time Mr Mahon too, was very weak from dysentery. However, God answered prayer for them all and healed them. The rattle of small artillery was constant. Often bombs would shriek overhead to scatter death and destruction in the neighbourhood. Yet God kept these, His children, in simple happy trust. The Mahon brothers now took part in the Red Cross work and had many opportunities to minister to the sick and dying.

A miller, to whom they had taken a nearly full bag of maize, exchanged this bag for half a bag of ground maize meal. We must record a most miraculous provision of God in connection with this bag. Mrs Mahon would send a plateful to her mother each week. Each week her mother remarked, "Surely this must be the last from your bag!" It was rationed daily to the members of the family and at times it was served to sick soldiers. A convalescent soldier who stayed in the home shared in the food of the family. Weeks wore into months. Hopes of coming relief were dashed to the ground again and again. Some even longed to fall into the hands of the enemy. Yet that half-bag of maize meal continued to

---

[26] $1.35.

provide nourishment for the family and others. It was not until the besieged were relieved by the British troops on 28 February 1900, that the half bag of meal was finished. This was as great a miracle as the widow's cruse of oil in Elijah's day, and a modern testimony to the faithfulness and all-sufficiency of God.

When the siege of Ladysmith was raised, God again provided in a wonderful way: A government supervisor of cattle saw Mr Mahon riding past with some horses one day. This man asked if Mr Mahon would trade those horses for cattle, adding that the government was in dire need of horses. Mr Mahon saw that there was good business in this. During the war, he had been employed by the YMCA and had managed to save most of his earnings. He now saw an opportunity to invest his savings in a profitable way. He bought and sold many horses and later used the profit as a down payment on some farmland he purchased.

48

Chapter 6

Blessing at Harrismith

The siege was over but the war continued for another two years. The Mahon family took up temporary residence on a deserted farm. Later they moved to a native reserve, witnessing and winning souls everywhere, praying for the sick and encouraging God's children to a simple trust in Him.

Chief Khumalo welcomed them and when the old chief was dying, God raised him up and added ten years to his life. This man had heard the testimony of God's power to heal and later, when he became very ill with rheumatic fever, he sent for Mr Mahon, saying, "I have asked my own folks to pray for me but they are so full of unbelief that they try to keep me back." Mr Mahon went to him and prayed for him. He was instantly delivered and became a loyal friend and helper of the work. The Khumalo family had magnificent voices and delighted in singing God's praises together as a family choir.

Living a day at a time, the Mahons were learning valuable lessons of trust in God alone. It was a hard school through which they were going, but looking back on it in later years, they said they would not have had it otherwise. God blessed them and used them, moulding them for larger service. They gained an insight into native customs and outlook, and their sterling qualities of friendship and generosity appealed to those among whom they took up temporary abode.

For those who had known the refinements of European civilization, these hardships meant a very real daily "taking up of one's cross," yet in later years all the Mahon children were able to take the responsibilities of the work with a rare understanding learned during the months of privation and war.

So far had the reputation of the Mahons gone ahead of them that when eventually they set out on an evangelising trip into Basutoland[27], the natives gathered from near and far. They came in great crowds to hear the gospel. They stormed the wagons with their maimed and sick for prayer. They brought presents of sheep and eggs. They spoke to Mr Mahon in affectionate terms of his father Alfred Mahon, the transport driver, whom they had known in the more leisurely days before the gold rush, and they begged the missionaries to establish stations among them.

Wherever they went, God confirmed their preaching with miraculous signs following.

There was a local Methodist preacher named Dhlamini, who was paralysed from his waist down. He had to be carried to the platform and be seated in a chair to preach. This man was brought to the meetings in a wagon. He was quite helpless. He had heard what God was doing, and came in simple faith. He was prayed for and was healed at once. He went back to his congregation at Driefontein, and leaped and ran before them to show how God had delivered him. This brought great blessing to the Methodist cause there and many were converted to God.

A dumb man was brought in by his friends who asked prayer for him. Immediately the dumb spoke aloud. The

---

[27] Modern Lesotho.

people were so unprepared for this that they were frightened.

These are but a few of the hundreds who were healed in the name of the Lord Jesus.

At last the way was clear for the Mahons to return to Harrismith. The sick followed them, begging for prayer or testifying to God's delivering power, until they actually reached the station to entrain for the Orange Free State. Indeed, as the train moved out, the Mahons still continued to cry to God for healing upon these unfortunate natives until their voices could no longer be heard by the crowd.

Mr Mahon obtained a small farm from the townlands on a twenty-year lease, and at once began to make a home. He put up a neat little house and planted trees. This retreat they named "Hillside." To earn a living he worked at blacksmithing and farming.

The Mahons were not left tranquil for long, however, for all along the western borders of Basutoland and up into the mighty Drakensberg Mountains, the news spread and the natives flocked to Harrismith with their sick. Mr Mahon was careful not to pray with them until they had been well instructed in the way of salvation and had trusted in the Lord Jesus. His whole time was soon taken up with ministering, and the power of God rested mightily on this servant of His.

A woman named Madihotetso, wife of Chief Matadira, of Basutoland, had gone insane. Her people tied her up, put her in a wagon, and brought her to the "doctor." Mr Mahon explained that he was not a doctor, and took no fees, but prayed for people freely and the Lord Jesus healed them as He had always done. The chief and his escort stayed with the Mahons for a few days to receive teaching. Mr Mahon commanded them to untie the woman. At first they seemed afraid, but at length they complied, and set her free. Mr Mahon talked with her and then commanded the devils to come out in the name of the Lord Jesus. The woman fell, apparently senseless, and slept for hours, awaking completely restored.

This news spread. Many were saved. Chief Alexander sent his wife, who had been barren for ten years. After prayer she was healed, and all the region of Peka saw how God had worked, for within a year she became a mother. Carlisle, the son of another chief, was healed of insanity in answer to prayer.

Crowds came with wagons to hear more of this wonderful salvation, bringing their sick with them. For a time the white people objected, complaining that the Mahons were introducing so much sickness into the area, but when it was shown that the sick went away healed, they could say nothing. Poor Mamueletsi had, had nine children that either died at birth or soon afterwards. Her husband brought her to Harrismith and she was prayed for. She went home and some years later they heard from her husband that God had answered their prayer and that his wife had given birth to three healthy babies.

A devil-possessed girl was brought in chains. Previously she had been tied with heavy ropes but she had snapped them. At Mr Mahon's request, they loosed her, though they declared that she would do the missionary grievous bodily harm. However, the devils were cast out in the name of the Lord Jesus and she was healed. This girl had a twin sister, at home who was also insane. The parents had intended to bring her as well, but she had run away and they were unable to find her. They were overjoyed at the healing of their daughter and begged Mr Mahon to go home with them and pray for the other twin. He told them that if they would trust the Lord, they could pray right there and God, who sees everywhere, would heal her where she was. Such was their simple faith in God that as prayer was offered they believed that God had healed their other daughter too. On returning home they were not surprised to find the other twin at home and well. When they inquired as to when she had become better, they found that it was when prayer was made for her at Harrismith. These people had been heathen, but now the whole family was converted to serve the living God. Both girls eventually were happily married.

Eventually, the work became so strenuous that the missionaries gradually formed the plan of having certain great gatherings in which they could minister the Word to thousands at once, thus saving very much hard work, and at the same time, making it possible for all to become acquainted with the teaching simultaneously. Thus began the then famous quarterly meetings, in which huge crowds gathered at some pre-arranged spot for a few days of fellowship and testimony.

Here we must remind ourselves that it was not a very long time ago that the Basuto waged a very successful war against the Free State. People who remembered those bloody encounters were still alive, at the time of writing. Imagine, then, the effect upon the people of Harrismith, when one day they awoke to find great trains of Basuto wagons streaming along their roads, laden with people singing hymns. Some of these had evidently come several days' journey. They were carrying white flags in a token of peace, but who knew whether this might not be a ruse?

Scores of horsemen accompanied the wagons, their picturesque Basuto blankets flying in the wind. Then from another direction came a second huge train of wagons, like some vast snake winding its length toward their town, these were Transvaal Basuto. While from the East would come similar great groups of Zulus from Natal, all singing the songs of Zion and bringing their sick to be prayed for, or with convicted souls seeking salvation.

What amazing gatherings they were. The quiet little farming town had suddenly become the centre of religious revival. From early morning till late at night the teaching, singing, praying and testifying went on. News got out of devil-possessed folk made sane in Jesus' name, of the blind seeing and the lame walking.

Where would it all end?

Of course the Devil was busy. Rumours got into circulation that the wagons were filled with arms. Anyone who is used to native life could have contradicted this, for these black folk would not have brought their wives and little ones had they wanted to fight. However, the townsfolk begged their mayor and counsellors to visit the meetings and to see that all was safe.

These enlightened gentlemen were accustomed to dealing with drunken brawls between natives, with fights and factions. Here, however, was something that was altogether strange to them. There were some eight thousand in that vast congregation. Hereditary enemies like the Zulu and Basuto were worshipping side by side. There was not even a suggestion of ill feeling in the whole assembly. Oxen and sheep were provided for the visitors, but they brought most of the food themselves, or bought it at honest prices in the neighbourhood.

Men who had once been wild and brutal and dangers to any community, were now bowing their knees side by side in the name of the Lord Jesus, confessing their sins and telling of how God had changed their hearts. Miracles were being performed as though they were the most common events of the day. Wagons were bringing in the sick, and before long, they were well and praising God for ridding them of their pains. The inhabitants had feared an uprising, but here was the very remedy that was needed. 'Lions' were being changed into 'lambs'.

Only one more objection could be raised. Sanitary arrangements for the town of Harrismith did not include so huge a concourse. Would they leave the town-lands in a litter of rubbish, refuse and worse? To their amazement, these gentlemen had to admit that the 180 wagons filed away as peaceably as they had come. The people showed nothing but joy and good will throughout. There was not the slightest suggestion of lack of respect. Never had so orderly a crowd visited the town, and moreover, pits had been dug for the reception of every scrap of rubbish, even to the ashes from their camp fires. When all had gone, the campsite was as clean and sweet as when they had arrived. There had not been a single hitch, not a jarring note.

Naturally, Mr Mahon and the gospel which he preached, gained immensely in the estimation of these counsellors. A message that could transform savages into saints was to be encouraged. The people of Harrismith were told that they were fortunate in having such a splendid work going on among them, and fears were allayed.

Chapter 7

Churches Organized

It was never Mr Mahon's desire to establish an independent church. His objective was to evangelise and then send the converts to established churches.

In many cases, however, these converts went to societies that were spiritually dead. Naturally, a really alive Christian, who comes among such groups, is a thorn in everybody's side, and everybody is a thorn in his. He wants to separate himself from the world but here is the world in the church. Friction is bound to result and either they stifle his testimony or, if they cannot do this, they turn him out. Take a case in point:

Matthias Mabutyana had been trained as a schoolteacher and for years had done a good work in the schools. He then became very ill. He resorted to numbers of doctors, both native and white, but nobody could decide what his trouble was. They took his money, contradicted each other as to what the trouble was, and finally left him weaker and more helpless than ever. He had to give up teaching and came to penury. For five weary years the disease dragged on and he could do nothing.

Then there came to his town a walking-stick salesman by the name of Shabane, who preached the gospel wherever he went. When Shabane had first heard the gospel he had hardened his heart. His wife longed to be a Christian but he refused to allow her to take the step. Eventually, he had a very long period of illness. When he found that no earthly aid could avail, he turned in his extremity to God. At this time his kidneys and stomach were in terrible condition. At times, large quantities of foul-smelling pus would discharge from his nose and throat. This condition was so bad that nobody could stay in his hut because of the offensive smell. Shabane came in touch with Mr Mahon's preachers and he and his wife were saved and God graciously healed him. He then spent his time going from place to place, far afield, preaching Christ. He supported himself by selling walking-sticks.

Shabane told Matthias that there was a higher life, a place of victory over sin and of separation from all that grieved God. He also told him that the Lord Jesus could still heal the sick. The sufferer grasped at this like a drowning man at a life buoy. He asked Shabane for prayer and was healed. A few days later, Matthias was out in the fields ploughing, to everyone's amazement. He did not know to what group Shabane belonged; he only knew that Jesus Christ had made him whole. He welcomed the walking-stick maker into his home that he might hear more of this wonderful gospel.

To all who would listen, Matthias witnessed of the great joy in his heart because his sins had been forgiven and also he had victory over self and sin through Jesus Christ. Moreover, Jesus still had the power to deliver and heal. Many of the members of the mission of which Matthias was a member, had not forsaken their sins and thus became enraged with him. They brought him before a superior missionary. He was told to stop preaching these "false doctrines" and to chase Shabane away. Matthias replied, "I am only teaching what I find in God's Word and moreover, if Jesus Christ does not heal the sick, how is it that I am here before you, whole? As for chasing away Shabane, how could you expect me to do that when he has brought me healing in the name of the Lord Jesus after years of suffering?" They could not find any reply, but simply excommunicated Matthias. This same story could be repeated for hundreds of cases. Against his wishes, Mr Mahon realised that he would have to form some kind of fellowship into which these people could be received.

At the close of the year 1903, the Rev Daniel Bryant, who was in charge of churches in Johannesburg and Pretoria under an American board, was invited to come to "Hillside" to establish a Church. Mr Mahon had chosen men from the early converts who had been found faithful and suitable as assistants to carry on the work. Time had been set aside for the instruction and teaching of these men. These were now dedicated by Rev Bryant as workers. Although many of them were not educated, it was evident to all that they were filled with the Holy Ghost and with power. They were capably taking charge of the work as pastors, eager to teach others about the wonderful gospel of Christ, and eager to be taught. Time has proven that these steps were taken under the guidance of God. Mr Mahon showed that he trusted his workers and they proved that they were worthy of his trust. Growing in grace and in knowledge of the Lord as the years passed, these men became capable leaders and able men of God.

Since that time, this work has been connected with the Grace Missionary Church of Zion[28], Illinois, USA.

---

[28] Now known as Christ Community Church. ZEMA (Zion Evangelical Ministries of Africa) is their missionary arm that oversees the work in Africa.

Chapter 8

Five Years at Kalkoenkrantz

The little farm of Harrismith town-lands soon became too small for the requirements of this rapidly spreading work. Mr Mahon looked about for a more suitable place. About twenty miles away was a larger tract of land which was for rent. It was unimproved but eminently suitable. The Mahons made it a matter of prayer and asked God's guidance. It was not long before a man came to lease the little farm at "Hillside" and paid the Mahons for all the improvements they had made there. Now, the Mahons had the means to pay for the lease of the larger farm, Kalkoenkrantz. Taking his son, Alfred, Mr Mahon went without delay to start building. They made mud bricks and soon had a building erected – the church building. The family was brought and lived in this building while a dwelling house was built. Mr Mahon continued to blacksmith and farm to support his family, but the growing spiritual work demanded most of his time.

One of his neighbours said that Mr Mahon had an immense respect for his Lord's command to go into all the world and preach the gospel. His life was one long "GO." At times when funds were low, he would take in blacksmithing work for the farmers around, working at this until noon on Saturday, after which he would harness up a wagon and set out to preach. Often he would continue preaching all through Saturday night and Sunday, returning late on

An ox-wagon crossing a stream

Sunday evening to snatch a few hours' rest before starting again at his forge on Monday morning.

This work was not allowed to interfere with his ministering and prayer. This neighbour testified, "The Mahons did not stop to ask how to go, where to go, or who would provide the money for going. They simply went. I never heard them beg, or even hint, yet it was very clear that they only had the barest necessities of life. They were capable as a family, and might well be wealthy, yet they kept pressing forward in the Lord's work with every resource they possessed. Their one boast was that God had never failed to send them food, clothing and a roof over their heads."

Many of the white neighbours were anything but sympathetic, but one little lad of about ten years saw things which made a lifelong impression on him. There was a daily prayer meeting and as soon as the bell rang, Mr Mahon went to pray. He did not stop to take the ploughshare or the horseshoe from the forge. That lad became a preacher of the gospel and he said that he is confident that the reason that Mr Mahon's work was so mightily blessed that it had begun and carried on in prayer. He concluded by saying, "I have known many men, but in my thirty years' experience, I never knew one who had so great and good an influence on both blacks and whites as Mr Mahon, and that influence is the power of the Holy Spirit, maintained through faithful prayer."

A man came in one day to ask Mr Mahon for the loan of a buck sail (a big stretch of canvas), to cover his wagon, as he was going to Bible conference.

The little boy thought, "Now we will see what this man of God will do!"

Mr Mahon said, "I have only one buck sail, just big enough to cover my wagon, and as I too am going to the conference I shall need it."

The man said, "Then I must be going."

"No! Wait a minute", said Mr Mahon, and went off. Presently he came back with a piece of canvas in his hands. It was half the buck sail. He could not bear to see his neighbour go off without shelter from the sun, and so he had unlaced the buck sail down the centre and was prepared to use only half in order that the other man might also be sheltered. Once more the little eyes took in the gracious deed, and a lifelong impression was made for God.

When overseer Bryant joined hands with Elder Mahon, the former promised that he would send out reinforcements from America, to take part in this great work. In this he was successful, for by degrees, several workers came from the Grace Church in USA, and from allied assemblies.

The question will naturally arise: How is it possible that, in a country like the Orange Free State, where there were Bibles in every home, and churches in every little village, that the native population should be neglected and left in heathen darkness? The only answer that one can give, and it is given with shame, is that these white people were contented to enjoy the solaces of the gospel themselves, but were absolutely without interest in making it known to the black folk who worked for them.

In times past, the struggle between blacks and whites put an antagonism into the hearts of both, and this abominable thing was allowed to continue. There were those who even dared to say that they did not wish to see their servants converted, for a Christian native is spoiled for further service. As though the gospel of the Lord Jesus ever spoiled anyone!

One white farmer told us, "As soon as these natives get converted they are tidier in their clothes, neater in their habits, cleaner in their homes, more humble in their demeanour. They become diligent, obedient and happy. Why, even their bodies seem to become healthier, their step more springy, their actions more lithe. They sing about their duties. They discard cheap jewellery and bangles, but they wear an air of sweet dignity which is far more attractive. Indeed, though it is not easy to describe in a few words, yet the change is unmistakable, and we say instinctively: 'That native has joined Mahon and become a member of his mission.' We can only remark as Mr Mahon himself would, 'He has joined the Lord Jesus and become a member of His mission.'"

In centres like Bloemfontein, one could find scores of different denominations at work in the one location, "sheep-stealing" from one another and with converts going where they could gain the greatest temporal advantage. Out on the eastern section of the Free State however, very little was done at all for the spiritual upliftment of the black people, and excepting for the very occasional visits of some itinerant native preacher, the servants on the farms were left absolutely in heathen blindness. The appalling degradation, the brutal heathen customs that prevailed there, and the darkness of ignorance and superstition were comparable to those in the worst parts of Africa.

Thus the new Mission, under Mr Mahon, was not encroaching upon the sphere of influence of other groups when it established at Kalkoenkrantz. On the other hand, a tremendous opposition was aroused from those who ought to have been saving the natives but were not doing so.

With regard to the use of means, while it was regarded as evincing a more simple faith in the healing power of the Lord Jesus when the sufferer abandoned all human aids, yet it was not felt necessary to denounce doctors and their efforts at alleviating sickness, or even to command the sick to abandon such means. The great thing was to demonstrate that Jesus Christ was the same yesterday, today and forever.

It was here that Edgar Mahon decided that he would gather together all the Christians who could attend, to have three days of intensive teaching. It was agreed that the most suitable time would be over Christmas.

They prepared for a large crowd but were simply overwhelmed when they saw the tremendous response. The people came from miles around on horseback, in ox-wagons and on foot. This proved so successful that the Christmas meetings were a great feature of the work. The attendance at times was over two thousand Christians.

Eventually it became evident that, once again, they must have a place of their own instead of submitting to the constant uncertainties connected with hired property. The missionaries again prayed that God would direct them to a property that they could make their own, a home that the missionaries and natives alike would regard as their headquarters.

The Lord guided them to a place called "Mooigelegen." Mr Mahon had just sufficient funds to make a down payment on this farm. He had to take a large bond on the property and wanted to make sure that there would be a portion for the Mission, if he should be unable to meet the bond and so lose the farm. He therefore set aside a few acres of the ground which he donated to the Mission. This became the nucleus of the Mission Station – "Etembeni."[29]

The native people were very happy because now they had a place of their own to gather at will, to worship God and be taught. Mr Mahon told his native workers that he planned to erect a church building on the mission lot. Gladly and happily they brought their offerings and gifts. It was largely through the gifts of the natives that the church building was erected. With the help of his son Alfred, Mr Mahon also built a cottage there, to house the first missionaries that came from Grace Missionary Church.

---

[29] Modern spelling: "Ethembeni". Located 50km north-west of Harrismith. (S 27° 58' 46.176'' E 28° 39' 36.43'').

Chapter 9

Headquarters at Mooigelegen

A favourite remark of Mr Mahon's was, "In heaven we shall get plenty of rest. Now is the time to work." And he set a perfect example. While buoyant about tasks already accomplished, he never allowed them to dull his sense of the great need still ahead.

In his ever-widening journeys, Mr Mahon began to make use of a big tent for evangelistic services. The workers would visit about three different neighbourhoods in the course of a week. The labour of packing and unpacking and erecting the tent was considerable. The uncertainties of this wondering life made it very arduous. However, the workers never wavered since they found it the most profitable method of spreading the blessed news of God's redeeming love.

Everywhere, praying for the sick proved to be the key which unlocked the hearts of men and women to the gospel message. Much time and care was given to Bible teaching before the sufferers were considered ready for such ministrations as the laying-on of hands in the name of the Lord Jesus. We believe that this preparatory teaching was the reason that so many very outstanding cases of healing constantly took place.

Violent opposition met the missionaries as the natives gathered for the meetings on the new farm. White people spoke of the possibilities of spreading disease, of bringing undesirable characters to the neighbourhood and of lowering the prestige of the white race. They found a great many other grounds for objecting to the mission farm. There were those who even refused to give their natives the usual written passes, permitting them to go to the services. Some natives were forbidden to attend the meetings. Others were turned back from the public roads, when they wished to go to Mooigelegen. Some suffered violence, yet they returned good for evil and respect for invectives.

The white farmers in the district were bitter about Mr Mahon preaching to the natives[30], and treated them with utter contempt and openly showed their hatred. The Mahon children were belittled and held up to scorn at school. The natives were abused for attending their meetings. All sorts of infamous falsehoods were circulated concerning the work. The white workers were ostracised and scorned. Public insult and private innuendo were heaped upon them, yet they were careful to return respect for reproach and kindness for hate, until those who were most in opposition had to cease for shame.

In this matter, great ground was gained by Mr Mahon's charming courtesy and kindness, while Mrs Mahon's practical help and neighbourly sweetness made a lasting impression. They were advertising the gospel of Christ as no pulpit oratory could ever do. Perhaps the greatest factor in changing the attitude of the neighbours, however, was the conversion and healing of a Mrs Leopold of Senekal and her subsequent death. This lady had lost both her husband and child. She had belonged to the Dutch Reformed Church, and in her hour of need and deep calamity the Mahons opened

---

[30] The first edition used the pejorative term for natives that the farmers would have used.

their home to her. Her miraculous deliverance from certain death from cancer and her new-found joy in the Lord Jesus made her wish to associate with those who had been a blessing to her. Thus she offered to teach spinning and weaving to the native school children.

Later, during a visit to Johannesburg, she was suddenly stricken with heart trouble and dropsy, which paralysed her lower limbs. Mrs Mahon's mother, Mrs Buchler, was a certified nurse, and went at once to Johannesburg. With infinite tenderness she brought the sufferer back to the farm. Mrs Leopold received every attention, but the Lord was calling and man could not refuse. She died rejoicing in the Saviour's grace.

Since this lady was Dutch[31], the Mahons sent to all the Dutch neighbours in the vicinity, inviting them to attend the funeral. All who came were struck by the kindness and courtesy of the missionaries. The friends spoke freely of their surprise that the Mahons would accept and nurse so tenderly a comparative stranger. They admitted that the false rumours that had been circulated were without foundation. Their attitude changed to one of admiration and respect.

One Dutch farmer, who had been the instigator of the false rumours of hatred and ill-will, came to Mr Mahon weeping and asked forgiveness. From that time on, this old gentleman became one of the staunchest moral supporters and friends of the Mahon family. Real conversion, and restitution so far as possible, for wrongs committed, were faithfully taught. This produced fruit which the most obdurate opponent could not deny.

Ndlebe came under the Gospel's influence and turned to the Lord Jesus while working for another farmer. He became

---

[31] The "Dutch" were of Dutch decent but would later be known as the "Afrikaners". The Dutch language in South Africa had already begun to evolve into what now is "Afrikaans".

most uncomfortable about his past thefts. Each time he knelt to pray, the sheep that he had taken would come before him. In South Africa the laws for stock theft were very severe and punishment very heavy, so Ndlebe was in agony of soul. He did not know how to act. At last he decided that at all costs he would put the matter right. He returned to his former master, confessed his thefts and concluded, "Here I am, sir. Beat me, imprison me, or do what you will. I am determined to be right with God and will make good what I have stolen as soon as I am able."

The owner of the sheep was so struck by Ndlebe's genuineness that he not only forgave him, but took him back into his employ and gave Ndlebe a far higher and more responsible position than he had held before.

Developments moved rapidly at Etembeni. The native children came from near and far to attend the school that was opened. Eagerly they grasped at the knowledge of being able to read their Bibles in their own language and to write. A neat school building, a church, a girl's boarding school and dwelling houses for the white missionaries were speedily erected.

Camp meeting

When the first two lady missionaries arrived from Grace Missionary Church, one of them took charge of the school. Many of the students were converted, and the influence of the missionaries made a lasting impression on them. Some of the young men became workers in the Mission and others became teachers.

On one occasion the Government inspector came to see what was being done and to decide whether the school could be declared worthy of a government educational grant. So struck was this gentleman with the good work that was being accomplished, that he not only recommended the grant in question but also added a substantial gift from his own pocket.

From time to time we found, among the speakers at the great camp meetings, ministers from the different white churches, two mayors of the Orange Free State towns, and half a dozen or more prominent chiefs from Zululand and Basutoland.

A little stream runs through the lower part of the Mooigelegen farm. This stream as well as scores of streams and rivers all over South Africa, saw glorious baptismal services.

Each month a letter is sent to every outpost of the work with news, teaching and encouragement for all. The local preachers and workers helped to circulate the letter among

A typical baptism

the believers, who looked forward to it with great eagerness. This later developed into a quarterly magazine which was published in three native languages.

The work on the farm was strenuous enough in itself. Mr Mahon cultivated wheat, maize, and oats. He was adept at breaking horses and trek-oxen. At times he also did a little wagon-making, at which he was very skilled.

Much of the year, however, saw him far afield with tent and wagon. His growing family threw themselves whole-heartedly into the work. Such incidents as the following were rarely recorded, though they formed the ordinary routine of Mr Mahon's life in seeking for God's lost sheep:

He was far from home, and night found him soaked with rain, arriving at the hut of some of the believers. No other quarters were available, and he had to have somewhere to dry his clothes. The hut was about fifteen feet in diameter. His roommates were the head of the family and his wife, an old man who was a family friend, the eldest daughter and her husband, four grown-up young girls, two young boys, two young calves, two cats and one hen with a brood of chickens – seventeen lives in all, not counting the chickens.

Needless to say there was not much sleep for Mr Mahon that night. When the calves did not bellow the cats mewed, the hen clucked, or somebody snored or spoke in his sleep. The calves were the noisiest sleep-mates of all, and he was glad to get home the next day. Journeyings, privations, weariness, exposure to the extremes of heat and cold, and above all the great burden of the care of the Churches, these were the badges of apostleship worn by Mr Mahon and his band of workers.

Thank God for the wonderful change in lives made by the gospel and by contact with Christian people. Still, however, the most terrible cruelties and puerile superstitions flourished. Tshaka's[32] wild orgies of blood often took place. His fierce warriors spread death and destruction over vast districts of southern Africa and they were never satiated in their awful blood lust. A warrior who returned home without his spearhead bathed in human blood was slain as a coward, and a regiment that suffered defeat was massacred. Thus, everyone's safety lay in strength of limb and agility. Men, women and children were slaughtered in cold blood. Tshaka once tested the bravery of his army by ordering a lion to be caught alive without a scratch to the animal. Many brave warriors were mauled to death before the wild monster was dragged before the monarch. Others suffered lifelong injury and pain to meet his whim.

On the death of Tshaka's mother, orders were sent throughout the land to bring in the most beautiful young women to be buried alive with her in order that the country might mourn, as it had never done before. Tshaka however, did not shed a tear.

It is related that Tshaka once saw a very deep ravine and wondered how many people it would take to fill it. To satisfy his curiosity he ordered his men to kill people and throw them in until the ravine was full. Fortunately, before he carried out this brutal design, his two brothers killed him. His murder was a relief to all.

How does this affect the story that we are telling? It simply shows the mentality of these people without Christ. Even today[33], ritual murder is rife. A missionary told us of a case where three charred bodies were found in a burnt hut. It was

---

[32] Also known as Shaka Zulu (c.1787 – 1828) was the most powerful and vicious of all Zulu monarchs. He molded the relatively small Zulu army into the most powerful fighting force in Southern Africa and expanded the Zulu kingdom dramatically through constant war and subjugation. His area of influence included the area where the Mahons worked.

[33] 1936.

discovered that they were the victims of a witch doctor. In order to cure a sufferer he said that he must have parts of three human beings. These parts must be hacked from the bodies while still living, so part of a little child's skull and pieces of the bodies of two women were cut away. Imagine the awful suffering involved! Then, to cover up his crime, the bodies were put into a hut and the thatch set on fire that it might appear that the three victims had been caught in the hut by accident and burned to death.

The gospel is declared to be "God's power for the salvation of everyone that believeth." Can it touch such depravity as this? Thank God, today there are thousands who have heard the gospel through the Mahon Mission, who are living testimonies that all can see. They evince, by devoted lives of love and self-denial, the change that the Lord Jesus has wrought.

One old farmer declared, "I have known Mr Mahon since 1912. I have watched the amazing change that his message produces. At first I opposed him, believing that he would spoil the natives. Never did I make a greater mistake. I trust those blacks with all my farm and business. They never steal or take advantage. As servants they are all I could desire. However wild and bad a criminal, a rascal, an outcast from society, as soon as he comes under the influence of that gospel message he is a changed man. All my farm workers are Mahon's Christians. When a neighbour complains of his servants, I tell him to get one of Mahon's Christians and he will have no more trouble."

Another said, "They never drink or smoke. They are always respectful, obedient and happy. Directly a native joins these people you can tell it at once, for his grumbling gives way to singing." Another gentleman said, "I rented Kalkoenkrantz after Mr Mahon left it. The little raw-brick chapel that he built is still standing. I leave it there as a monument to the splendid work done by the Mahon Mission. I believe it will stand for a century."

It is significant that years after the headquarters was moved from Harrismith, so great was the respect which the towns-people had gained for Mahon that they gave an official invitation to him to hold another great camp meeting in their townlands. It brought much good and blessing to the whole community. This invitation was gratefully accepted and preparations were made for the Christmas meetings there. What amazing gatherings they were! The quiet little farming town had suddenly become the centre of a religious revival. From early morning till late at night the teaching, singing, praying and testifying went on.

Chapter 10

The Testimony Spreads in Natal

We have seen how God blessed Mr and Mrs Mahon in Natal, how hundreds flocked to the banner of Christ, and how the sick were miraculously delivered. At that time the work was enriched by some of the most staunch and capable of its native workers. Let us follow one of them, Timothy Mabuza, a Methodist evangelist, and by birth a Swazi.

He had heard Mr Mahon preach at Harrismith in 1902 and the message had struck deep into his heart. The preacher had said, "You come here to see in me a prophet or a healer, but I am neither. I am a simple preacher of the gospel and come to urge you to trust in God who is able to save your souls and heal your bodies."

Mabuza went home and told his wife of hearing a preacher who had stirred his heart. He told of the miracles of salvation and healing that he had seen. His wife was unmoved. About three months later their son was bitten by a poisonous snake, while away in the mountain. Mabuza prayed for the son. A bite from this snake, a puff-adder, means quick death. The lad's body started to swell, blood was coming from his nose, but the power of God prevailed, and the son was restored. This convinced Mabuza's wife. She accepted Christ as her Saviour and they both were baptized.

Mabuza began to preach to his congregation about Christ's redemptive and healing power. Like Mr Mahon, when taken to task by his superiors, Mabuza preferred to resign. He was well loved by his people, so some of his congregation followed him and they joined with the Mahon Mission.

At Mangweni, a native reservation in the Estcourt District of Natal, most of the people were heathen and took pride in the fact that they followed the ways of their forefathers. They did not want the 'white man's religion' since it interfered with their tribal customs. Christians did not take part in the old heathen ceremonies and ways of living.

Nonqai Mazibuko was one of the tribe. He was well known for his bravery and was a fine strong young man, well versed in all the social customs. He was admired by all of his group. He had been married for only a few years and was the father of one child, a little girl, whom he loved dearly. It was a sad day for him when she became so ill that even though the witch doctor was called in, nothing brought relief. Nonqai became desperate. He tried white doctors but still the little one did not recover. He was determined to find out who could cure his little girl.

News quickly spreads among the Africans, and if anything out of the ordinary happens, it does not take long until something is known of it. So they heard of Mr Mahon who was preaching the gospel over a hundred miles away. Nonqai also heard that Mr Mahon prayed and the sick were healed. This was a long way to take a little sick girl. However, there was a man named Mabuza who was a follower of Mr Mahon, and he was only fifty miles away. Nonqai would go to Mabuza and find out for himself.

Taking his wife and child, Nonqai started on the long journey on foot. Fortunately, the people were very hospitable in those days, and the little party found food and shelter at night. They were warmly welcomed at Mabuza's home. Soon the weary travellers were fed and rested. Mabuza explained the way of salvation to them but they were not interested. All they had come for was to have their child healed. Here this man was saying that God could not heal their child if they were going to continue in their heathen ways. Moreover, this man would not accept any fees from them. They were puzzled. Mabuza, meanwhile, sought the Lord for this couple in earnest prayer. Gradually the light dawned on their darkened souls, and they joyfully accepted Christ as their Saviour. Then Mabuza prayed for the little girl and told them that God would honour their trust in Him. Nothing happened at that time, but as they journeyed home the child began to mend, and slowly complete healing came.

Just as faithfully as Nonqai had served the world, he now served his God. He invited Mabuza to come and preach the gospel in his hut and invited all his old friends to come to hear the great news. Two of his friends, Vilakazi and Dhlangalala, were converted. The heathen were stirred to the quick. Here was something creeping in that was violating their traditions and customs. They must get rid of this Mabuza. On his next visit to this village Mabuza was attacked with sticks and spears. He had to flee for his life. He escaped by hiding in thickets and creeping along riverbeds. He was forbidden to come to the village again by Nonqai's elder brother, the head of the family.

Other doors were opened and Mabuza was blessed of God as he risked his life to preach the gospel. Many were converted. He invited Mr Mahon to come over and assist in the work. It was not possible for Mr Mahon to go but he sent Cyril Cornell who was assisting him at the time. Alfred Mahon was sent along as interpreter. The meetings were well advertised, and many came to hear the words from these white men. There were several women who had been convicted under Mabuza's preaching. Their husbands came with them, not to listen, but to keep watch over their wives to keep them from becoming Christians.

Much prayer had preceded these meetings. As the people gathered by the hundreds, the Spirit of God was working. While the midday service was in progress, many were moved to tears. The preacher announced, "We will sing the hymn *Wazithwal Izono, Yesu Wazithwal' izono*" (You Bore Our Sins, Lord Jesus). While we sing this hymn, will all those who wish to accept Christ Jesus as their Saviour make their way to this altar." The people rose to sing. Their voices could be heard a long way off. Before the first verse was finished, some women had come forward and were kneeling at the altar. A number of men rushed forward, angry and ready to fight. They grabbed the women and tore the clothes from their backs. Mr Cornell made a move to protect the women, but Mabuza tapped him on the shoulder and quietly said, "Look up." Prayer saved the situation. The men were unable to drag the women away. With torn clothing they continued to kneel in prayer and consecration to God. The men saw that it was no use trying to drag their women away so they left them there. They would be dealt with at their homes. But all the beatings the women received did not prevent them from attending services.

In due time a baptismal service was arranged. The husbands had said that there would be blood shed if their wives were baptized. Hundreds of people came to the river to see what would happen when the twenty candidates were baptized. One man came up to Alfred Mahon and, pointing to his heart with a stick, said, "You come here again and I will stab you here." As the candidates were about to enter the water a man rushed up to one of the women, brandishing his sticks. He never used them, however. His hands fell powerless to his sides and the sticks dropped out of them. The other men, seeing what happened, remained where they were and the service continued without hindrance.

For many years the Christians at Mangweni suffered persecution. Young girls were beaten by their parents, but the

Lord's work grew. The converts refused to make beer in their homes or to follow any of the heathen customs. Their steadfast faith in God eventually led to the conversion of some of the men, and resistance to the gospel meetings broke down.

In the years that followed, Timothy Mabuza was used of God to reclaim hundreds of drunkards, witch doctors and similar bad characters. Two of his relatives are glorious trophies. One was a raving maniac tied up with fencing wire because nothing else was strong enough to hold him. He was delivered and saved in the name of Jesus. This resulted in many turning to God. The other Mazibuko was a notorious thief. He stole sheep and goats and pilfered in the plantations. Nothing was safe from his light-fingers. However, he too turned to Christ, was born again, and is now living an honest Christian life.

The work spread by leaps and bounds. Mabuza took oversight from the south of the railway line to Durban and another stalwart named Zulu, to the north. Zachariah Zulu had been converted from heathenism. When he met Timothy Mabuza, the two men immediately became fast friends. Mabuza was filled to overflowing with love and joy. This had been a deep need in the life of Zulu. He became a co-worker of Mabuza, and God blessed their ministry in Natal.

Mabuza had a way of gaining the attention of his congregations by bringing them into good humour, then launching out with the gospel. When Zulu stood up to speak, he started in a quiet voice, but what force that man had! His words burned into the hearts of the listeners. To know Zulu was to love him. His life was given over entirely to the Lord. Like Paul, Zulu took with him a young worker as he walked from village to village spreading the good news of the gospel of salvation. The native people were hospitable and Zulu and his worker would spend several days at a village teaching and preaching and then moved on to the next village. He visited his converts regularly and taught them the Word of God, encouraging them in their Christian walk.

In Natal, a mission station must have a certain amount of farmland attached, for raising food. Now quite close to the mission station was the reserve of Chief Tatazela. It was a hotbed of the dissatisfied, the criminal and the sneak-thief. Alfred knew better than to avoid such people. They were the very ones he wished to win for Christ. "They that are whole need not a physician, but they that are sick." He was after sinners and here they were in abundance.

On the other hand it was most awkward when one's sheep and cattle disappeared overnight, and when one's property was not safe. For a time he would watch for the culprits, get them arrested and put in prison, thus attempting to stop the thieving. Instead of this it merely alienated the affections of the people from him. They would not listen to his message, and became even more determined in their attacks upon his property.

He was desirous above all things to do God's will, to win souls, and to keep their ears open to the gospel. Peter could cut off the ear of Malchus, but Christ would heal it. Thus Alfred made it known through his Christians that he would not take any further action against the thieves. If they wanted to carry off the whole place they could do so. He was leaving the matter in God's hands.

For a time the pilfering continued, but then it stopped altogether, and shortly afterwards the chief himself came to visit Alfred. The latter was busy for a while and did not recognise his visitor, but when he saw who it was waiting at his gate, he called him in, apologised for keeping him waiting, and they had a heart-to-heart talk.

The incidences of salvation and healing spread far and wide. This marked the commencement of an exceedingly fruitful period of evangelisation, so that the groups of believers were multiplied most gloriously.

Chapter 11

The Power of Song

One of the things that Mr Mahon missed after he left the Salvation Army was the band. The Army always had a band. He had a cornet, which he could play beautifully, but that was not suitable for teaching singing. He set about to remedy this. He procured a concertina and taught the natives to sing. This was simple enough as they loved singing and it was not long before choirs were formed in all parts of the work. Choir singing was always an integral part of the Mission. Mr Mahon would go preaching the gospel by ox-drawn wagon and would take a small choir along. When he stopped for the night while camp was being set up, he would get out his concertina and the choir would sing. In no time at all there would be a curious and interested crowd. How simple it was after they had enjoyed the music and song, to tell of a Saviour who loved them and had died for them.

Mr Mahon loved people and always took a deep interest in them. This love drew men to him. A great part of his ministry was personal work. He often went into the late hours of the night, dealing with individuals and teaching the way of salvation. In this way, many were won to the Lord. Choir practices were attended with the same seriousness as Bible readings and prayer meetings. It appeared as natural for these converts to break into song as for the birds.

Wherever the missionaries went they were accompanied by a male quartet or a choir of five or six voices. Their use as a soul-saving agency was as powerful as that of the preacher. Again and again hard hearts were melted into repentance and salvation by the singing of the gospel. Imagine Mr and Mrs Mahon going in one direction, with tent and motor lorry, while Mr and Mrs McCordic set out in another, with their equipment. Each was accompanied by a choir of earnest soul-winners, who were prepared to do personal dealing. Most of them were young and eager. They assisted in erecting the tent and bringing the people in.

At the centres where they ministered, the people were captured by the hymns. The gospel strains were infectious and hundreds of people took up the song as the group moved about the country. A poor man in a crowded congregation mutters in a frightened voice, "Let me get out of this tent before they sing that chorus again or I shall have to turn from sin to God." Fortunately, the crowd was too dense for his exit, and before the chorus were finished, he rushed forward to the penitent form instead.

A choir

The natives composed some of the tunes. They hung on to the chords as to some toothsome morsel, rolling them on and on. Tears ran down black cheeks and Christ found His way into hearts and lives.

The relatives of one woman were praying much that God would save her soul during the visit of the preacher to their village. She vowed that she would not go near the tent, but when the choir started as a signal that the service was commencing, she was irresistibly drawn. Before she knew what she was doing, she was sitting with the rest. The message stabbed her heart. She knew she ought to be saved and she had heard the way of salvation. All that was needed was some power to break down her resistance. She was never absent from the meetings, but she never let down her shield of stubborn opposition. At last the services were over and the last benediction pronounced. This woman was on the point of yielding. Somebody asked for just two more hymns before the truck was to leave. That woman could not stand against those two extra hymns. She fled. Her relatives followed and found her hiding beneath a blanket in a neighbouring hut. "Don't let me hear that hymn," she cried, trying to stop her ears with the blanket. But the sweet voices of the choir floated into the hut. She was spellbound. Before the last verse was sung she was back in the tent, crying to God to forgive her and cleanse her guilty soul. The song had captured her for Christ.

The gospel band had, had a weary day, packed full with service for the Lord Jesus. They came to a spot that was eminently suitable for camping. All the younger members of the band prepared to unload the motor truck and start an evening service. It would make a convenient place to rest on their way to Standerton, which was their goal. However, the Spirit told Mr Mahon to move on farther.

Near sunset they came to a halt. Mr Mahon led the choir, singing and playing his concertina. They sang a well-known hymn. At once the people came running. They seemed to appear from nowhere. Soon there was a great crowd. They took up the strains of the hymn and flung it broadcast on the winds. What a glorious ending to their day! The people were ready for the message now. The singing in the Spirit had enthralled them, and they drank in the word of salvation.

Early the next morning a white man came to inquire, "What was that wonderful music? My wife and I were enjoying the cool of the evening when we heard angelic music. Oh, it was wonderful!" The missionaries were invited to breakfast. The white man slaughtered a sheep for the natives. He was a believer and was filled with joy at this unexpected fellowship. He followed the gospel party to Standerton and helped them in the witness there, throwing himself into the ministry with zest. Had it not been for the timely leading of God's Spirit and for the sweet evening song, that man would never have enjoyed that precious spiritual uplift.

During the special times of quarterly conferences the choirs all came prepared to sing. Some of them sang beautifully. Others did not have the advantage of good teachers to instruct them. Songs were sung in Zulu, Sesotho, English, and Dutch, with a versatility that was remarkable. Some of the men had magnificent bass voices and might have made names for themselves as professional singers. Not only was it expected that choir members would first be converted but also that they would show lives of devotion to the Lord Jesus.

We were touched by an old man of about eighty years who had travelled five long days over the mountains to have fellowship with the children of God. He was accompanied by two old, wrinkled women of about the same age as he. They were standing alone in the midst of heathen darkness up there in a mountain village of Basutoland; but not to be outdone, they, too, stood and with trembling voices sang their choir piece – four verses of it, gaining confidence with each succeeding verse and no doubt giving a testimony that would sink as deeply into hearts as that of any of the younger folk with their richer, clearer tones.

Chapter 12

The Gospel Spreads to the Mountains of Basutoland

It was only natural that the news of wonderful salvations and healings would spread into the farthest corners of the country. As a result of the testimony of Basutos who were being healed and saved, the most influential chiefs and headmen of Basutoland sent spies to attend the meetings and to bring back word as to whether the power of God was really accomplishing all that was reported.

These spies went back full of what they had seen and heard. An old, grey-haired man stood in one meeting, and told how he had spent most of his life as a witch doctor, but now God had made him ashamed of his deception. He had heard that "Without are dogs, sorcerers, fornicators, murderers, idolaters and everyone that loveth and maketh a lie." He had been afraid to doctor his own relatives and children, for he knew it was all a fraud. He now turned to Christ for deliverance and forgiveness. Then a girl who had been trained as a witch rose and confessed her sin and turned to God. After that, a local preacher from another mission rose and told how he had lived an unclean life but was sick of hypocrisy. He wanted deliverance. These were real, living issues.

Two men were preaching in one place, and many were being converted. Some married women were saved and their husbands were furious. They entered the tent, stripped the women of their clothes, and endeavoured to drag them from their knees. These men flourished their assegais[34] threateningly. One man was about to intervene, but the old native preacher Mabuza, said, "No, sir, don't raise your hand. Let God work." They prayed, and the men were at once rendered powerless to interfere further.

Next day there was a baptismal service, and the enraged husbands had vowed to stop it. Several young men were present, with shields in their hands. As the candidates stepped into the water, men rushed forward with sticks, to drag their wives out. However, as the Christians prayed the sticks dropped from the hands of the opposers, and they stood absolutely powerless to interfere further with the service.

A girl near Lichtenburg had run a broken needle into her hand, and though operated on many times by native and white doctors until her hand showed many scars of incisions, they could not get the needle out. It was lodged between the bones in the back of her hand, and X-ray photographs showed it was held so fast that removal would be impossible without breaking the bones. Her master, Mr Young, was a Christian, and had been blessed during services held by Mr Mahon in Bechuanaland. He suggested that she should send to Mooigelegen for prayer. A special day and hour were appointed, when the sufferer at one end of the country, and the missionaries at the other end, would unite in prayer. Within a day or two the needle worked out at the back of her hand.

Mia was furious when two of his wives were converted about the same time. He decided to kill both of them. Taking

---

[34] Zulu spears.

his knife and a rope, he called them to accompany him into the forest for firewood. Then when he had them alone he tied one up and prepared to cut her throat. The woman made not the slightest show of resistance. She stood like a lamb. The husband had expected a struggle, which would have warmed his temper to do the brutal act, but as she stood meekly before him he dropped his knife, saying, "I cannot do it. You stand there like an innocent sheep."

Sometime later he was journeying on horseback when he was struck to the ground by a brilliant light and converted to God. Returning to his wives, whip in hand, he appeared as if about to thrash them. How joyful they were when, instead of his showing them the usual cruelty, he dropped to his knees and begged them to pray for him.

On another occasion a man, paralysed for two years, was carried to the missionaries as they stood preaching. They taught him and then prayed for him. A month later news came that he was completely healed. Later, since he had made no move to repentance, a local preacher warned him most solemnly that he should not make light of what God had done for him, lest a worse thing come upon him. He became angry and shouted, "Go away with your God. I don't want Him." Immediately he fell sick, and died shortly after.

Naturally, such incidents as these made a tremendous impression on those who had come to "spy out the land." This was no mere theorising. The gospel was being demonstrated before them daily. They saw the incurable made well, the blind given sight and the lame walking. The news was carried back into the mountains. Here was a gospel with tangible results. God was working with these preachers and confirming their testimony by miracles and signs. As a result, a great longing was set up in the hearts of many. They must hear these words for themselves. They must ask the preachers to visit them.

It certainly seemed as though the Devil was working against his own interests when the witch doctor Mutseremedi Mataba one day presented himself at the Mooigelegen Farm, announcing that he had come from the wildest part of the mountains of Basutoland, and wished for someone to bring the gospel to his people at Sehonghong.

At Peka, where Chief Alexander's wife had been healed and she then had a child, the first meetings were held. God blessed in a wonderful way. Chief Alexander was converted. Many other saints were saved and some miraculous healings took place.

One day Mr Mahon was sitting in the open, in Basutoland, having breakfast with his faithful helper, Elijah Lutango when they saw a horseman coming toward them. He was a stranger and neither had seen him before, yet Mr Mahon said, "I want that young man for the gospel." He proved to be a chief, and his wife a chief's daughter. He held a position of great and growing importance, yet at the call of God he left all. His friends and acquaintances reviled him, scoffed at him and cajoled him by turns, hoping to turn him from his purpose, but this young chief, Samuel Molapo, put his wife and child on a horse, while he himself walked, and saying goodbye to all that the world holds dear, he travelled over one hundred miles to Mooigelegen Farm, to offer himself for the work. Since that time he was a tower of strength to the Mission and, though he had sacrificed a kingdom on earth, he was laying in spiritual store for a Kingdom that is eternal.

Unless one has seen the vast mountain ranges of Lesotho, it is difficult to believe that such scenery could exist. Wild peaks tower eleven thousand feet into the sky. Unscalable pinnacles rear their needlepoints among the clouds. Fantastic cliffs hang as though they might at any moment totter their thousands of tons of rock into the valley below. Torrents roar and waterfalls shower their spray into gloomy canyons.

Here and there among nature's grand confusion tiny horse tracks cling to the hillsides, skirt giddy precipices and wend their maze-like way to little Basuto hamlets, perched like eagles' aeries in the mountain crags. Secluded green vales offer pasturage to the herds of these hardy mountaineers. Shelters were built to protect them during the wild storms that swept those heights of the Maloti Mountains.

The reports of that needy land, and the longings of its villagers touched the heart of Evaline Mahon. As a girl of twelve she had begged her father to allow her to go into Basutoland and to preach to the people. Now she was a woman of twenty-four, and her father said: "My child, I only refused you before because you were too young. Now God forbid that I should keep you back from going where He is calling you." At that time, Miss Mahon had been training a choir at Mooigelegen for five years. They loved her and asked permission to accompany the party into the mountains.

The "Devil's Tooth" at Mont-Aux-Sources

Never before had Sehonghong seen such a cavalcade. There were twenty-seven horseback riders as well as several pack animals. The young men and women who accompanied the party had not sufficient saddles, but nothing daunted, they rode bareback, and with nothing but cured skin "riems"[35] for reins.

They were caught in a thunderstorm in the mighty mountain vastness. Before they could reach shelter they were all soaked. Eventually they gained a cave, where the party was able to wring water from clothes and get a little drier. However, Miss Mahon became so sick that for a time her condition seemed serious. They all cried to God, "Lord, if it is Thy desire that she should undertake this task, then set Thy seal upon it by delivering her." To everyone's joy healing came quickly, and the party was able to proceed.

How those choirs echoed in the mighty mountain precipices. How the people flocked to listen! They wanted to touch the white ladies: the first whom they had ever seen. They begged them to take off their shoes and stockings, to see if they had toes. Their hair was an object of continual wonder and admiration.

A Sehonghong village

---

[35] Leather ropes or straps.

It was to this isolated country that the gospel came and was joyfully received. The chief granted a site for a mission station and building operations began. Building occupied about four months under the supervision of Mr Mahon and party. All through May, June and July the snow fell heavily. At last when the building was finished, Mataba declared that there was a way by which they could get out of the mountains, and that he would give them guides and mules. The young guides seemed confident that they could guide the party out safely. Miss Mahon was left there alone, and Mr Mahon and his party set out bravely into the snow.

The passes were so blocked by drifts that in places the horses and mules sank to their girths, while the cold and cutting winds tried the little party to the utmost. However, they safely reached their stopping place for the night: a shelter that had been put up for the cattle herds. Here a warm spring yielded abundant fresh water, and camp was made.

This was one of the most isolated outposts in the mountains. During the night the snow fell and drifted so deeply that in the morning it seemed as though they were cut off before and behind. The party grimly faced the situation. To stay meant slow starvation, while to go seemed almost equally certain death in a whirling wraith of snow. Even their guides were at a loss. Only prayer could avail. They were travelling where, at any moment, a wrong step might take them over a precipice. Only the most venturesome would hazard their lives in those highlands, even in the best of weather. Now in the wildness of the storm, calamity seemed inevitable. At times, when they were doubtful, they would pray, commit their steps to God; then the foremost guide would plunge forward on his horse into the snow and the others would follow. At last they reached the source of the Tugela River and the edge of the vast Mont-Aux-Sources amphitheatre. They could actually see the hotel thousands of feet below but only seven miles away.

Frequently the velocity of the wind at this point was such that its moaning and shrieking could be heard a dozen miles away. Huge rocks were dislodged and hurled over the precipices. The little party realised that even a slight wind at this crucial moment could bury them entirely in the drifting snow. They halted just long enough to ask that God would still the wind until they could reach a sheltered spot. Even the guides marvelled. They were heathen men, but again and again they had to admit that God *was*, and that He was guiding their steps during that perilous descent. He was stilling the wind too. Eventually the faith of the missionary party was rewarded. They came out safely to the trading store of a Mr George Grey. This gentleman could hardly believe his eyes when he saw what those rugged mountains had given up. With awe he looked at the party as at those who had come back from the grave. Those at Mooigelegen Farm had seen the snow falling in the Basutoland mountains and had given up all hope of seeing their loved ones again. They shouted for joy when the party arrived safely.

When the party that had accompanied Miss Mahon eventually left, the people were amazed to see her start to set her little hut in order, commence enamelling her bedstead and plant flowers. They had thought that she would give way to wild weeping and grief, at being thus left alone among strangers.

Mutseremedi himself undertook to protect and provide for Miss Mahon. Two of his wives turned to the Lord Jesus, but he himself never made any confession of faith. A number of his family were saved. Assisted by three native Christian girls, Miss Mahon lived there for five years.

She lived chiefly on rice and eggs. Though Mutseremedi the witch doctor had promised to see that his missionary was well provided for, yet in practice, whenever he brought back a pound of tea, or a packet of sugar, from the outside world, his wives got most of it, and the poor missionary only received the leavings. She cultivated a small garden, and at times had lettuce. The herd boys stole most of her potatoes. Theft was considered no disgrace unless found out. One of the native women knew Zulu, and through her, Miss Mahon learned Sesotho. God honoured her testimony by saving very many.

The whole situation was most depressing. The country was overstocked with native herds, and consequently the best of the soil was constantly washed away by erosion. The natives only held their lands by very precarious tenure from the chiefs. Thus they never cared to enrich it, and merely lived from hand to mouth.

The missionary encouraged them to beautify their homes and make their sordid lives more comfortable. She found however, that the whole social structure was against her. When young men and women would come of age, they went to separate "heathen schools". Here they were not only taught interesting and useful things, but also many things that were sordid and wrong.

Young Christians who refused to consent to this were seized by force, beaten and abused until they submitted. Some young men ran to Miss Mahon for protection. She hid them and tried to help them to escape. However, they were caught, and she herself was brought before the chiefs on the charge of hiding and helping them. When she was about to answer the charges one young man himself turned on the older men and said, "You men took Mr Mahon by the hand, said you wanted the Christian religion, and promised to protect his daughter. Now that he has gone you endeavour to turn us from the Lord Jesus."

Then, taking out her Bible, Miss Mahon said, "Let us not banter words. I will read you God's Word, and show you what He Himself says." Immediately there was consternation. "Don't open that Book here," they cried. Indeed they seemed so fearful lest they should have to listen to God's

Book that the case was quashed, and Miss Mahon was allowed to go.

Mutseremedi's father Lihlohla Mataba was a thorough old gentleman, most benevolent to the poor, and always ready to help the missionaries. He had given Mr Mahon a white horse and a skin caross[36], as a token of his approval and friendship. When he fell ill, Miss Mahon went to nurse him and to pray for him until he was well on the road to recovery. There was a "heathen school" in progress close by, and the missionary was quite surprised when, in response to her request, they moved this assembly to another part of the village, that the old man might have a quiet night. All night long she prayed in a verminous hut close to that of the old man. Finally, they were able to rejoice in his deliverance. His daughter told the people that her father had seen a vision of the Lord Jesus dying on the Cross for him, and she urged them all to repent and turn to God.

On saying goodbye, Miss Mahon warned him against allowing any heathen customs to rob God of the glory of this

Miss Mahon's cottage in the mountains

---

[36] A treated animal-skin cloak or blanket with the hair still left on.

healing. However, as soon as she had turned her back they brought in the bone-throwers and witch-doctors, to "clear the hut of the white woman's spells." From that hour the old chief declined, and died soon after.

He had been a staunch friend of the missionaries, and was a man of his word. While he lived the white lady was well-cared for. She merely had to tell him, "There are certain poor folk yonder, who are suffering through the cold." It was sufficient. He would give orders for blankets to be taken from his store and carried to those in need.

With Mutseremedi it was quite different. He was immensely wealthy in cattle and sheep, but would not take the trouble to care for his white guest. If she needed a horse he would promise, "I will have one saddled and sent round to you," but she would wait in vain, until at last, tired of his thoughtlessness, she would call her native Christians together, and set out on foot, walking for days over those wild mountains, only to find later that the chief was vexed with her for having done so.

His sister had been head of a "heathen school" for girls. Her brother forbade her to become a Christian, but conviction was so deep that in agony of soul she would roll weeping in the dust. At last she defied her brother and the other elders, and took a bold stand for the Lord Jesus.

It was no easy task for a refined white lady to live among such heathen surroundings. At one time she was staying in a hut quite close to where about two thousand men had gathered for the feasting and drinking which concludes the initiation ceremony of the young men. The frenzied mob had threatened to set fire to her thatch roof, and with her faithful girls she stayed up all night to protect her hut from the sparks.

Another time she had to stay in a hut overrun with vermin, with a vomiting drunken woman on one side and another drunken woman on the other whose baby had whooping cough.

In spite of heathen feasts, often lasting for a week at a time, so close to her hut that the dancing and stamping actually shook the ground, God's protection was over her. Never once did anyone approach to do her harm.

The sight of her storm lantern, moving along the hillside, was the sign for evening meeting, and many loved to see its twinkle amid the darkness. One night some men planned to get this lantern for use in the foul rites of the heathen school. They came to ask for it with the excuse that it was to rescue a cow that had fallen into a pit. However, God turned even this to good account, for a young Christian man lay apparently dying, when he saw the light moving along the village. At once he took fresh courage. The power of God fell upon him, and those who were standing round, expecting his last breath, were amazed to see him sit up and start to preach to them. He had been healed on the spot.

Hundreds of souls were saved, and many were healed. The government officials however, were nervous about a white lady staying so far away from any help. The nearest white man lived at a trading store five hours' journey away by horseback. At times deep snowdrifts in the mountains isolated those villages from the outside world for months at a time. Thus the officials suggested that a site be chosen in a more accessible spot. A move was made to Chief Rafoletsane, who welcomed them gladly, and offered them a site for the building of a station. A teacher was left to care for the already established work.

It was thus that the gospel banner was planted among the mountains, and at the time of writing, glorious harvests of precious souls were being gathered in for the Lord Jesus.

Chapter 13

At the Lichtenburg Diamond Diggings

Was there ever a more desolate, hopeless region than that of the "proclaimed" diamond workings? Huge piles of gravel show where the soil had been worked. Here and there a winch dragged out fresh soil, while the prospector turned over every minute particle in his eagerness to find diamonds.

Tiny corrugated iron shacks were put up for the families of the miners. There were only the very barest elements of sanitation and practically no comforts.

Detectives, illicit diamond buyers, light-fingered natives and hard-boiled criminals rubbed shoulders. Everybody mistrusted everyone else, and life was one long disheartening scramble for gems. Men allowed their children to go in rags and their wives hungry while they scratched, day after day, turning over sieveful after sieveful, from first light until darkness made work no longer possible. Occasionally they would find some insignificant gem, and only very rarely indeed was a really valuable stone turned over.

Schoolmasters, prosperous farmers, professional men and down-and-outs thronged there together, in the gamble for easy wealth. They threw away their life's savings, broke up their homes, abandoned their families and soiled their souls in the quest for diamonds. It was like some hideous living octopus that gripped its tentacles on their lives, and there was no escape. "Once a digger always a digger" was the saying and it was almost invariably true.

The rarer stones were so uncommon that when a man really did find one he abandoned himself to an orgy of foolish spending, and in the end, found himself even poorer than before. It is estimated that there were some 7,000 whites and 20,000 to 30,000 natives on "the diggin's," and that not more than five per cent of them ever made anything out of it. Life was one long drawn-out forlorn hope, yearning for some rare gem. "A twenty carat blue" represented the highest goal of most men's ambitions. They gambled for it, sinned for it, despaired for it, and finally lost their grip of their lives and went off into the darkness of eternal doom with the magic formula still ringing in their minds "a twenty carat blue."

Of course the white man must have natives to help him, and it was quite probable that a large number of the natives, with sharp eyes and deft fingers, made more out of the diamonds than their employers could. These natives flocked to the

A digger's home

diggings from every tribe in South Africa. Many white men wanted their labour, but few indeed thought of their precious souls. These throngs of black folk offered a very real opportunity for Christ.

We have seen that Mr Mahon had already visited the Bechuana[37] on his way to Mashonaland[38]. Now the Basuto and the Bechuana were very closely allied. Lichtenburg was only thirty miles from the borders of Bechuanaland, and those people still weighed heavily upon his soul.

While the missionaries in Africa asked God to send workers to the diamond diggings, He answered thousands of miles away, in Iowa, USA. A young Christian named Fales was given visions of a needy people without a church or gospel message, waiting for his witness. So heavily was he weighed down by this vision that he offered himself to the mission, was accepted, and went to study with Mr and Mrs McCordic at Etembeni, where he met, and later married Margaret Mahon.

Trips were planned and evangelising visits were made to the diggings, but these only served to whet the appetites of the missionaries. For a time Elder Mahon even thought of selling out at Mooigelegen and buying a farm in the Lichtenburg area. No suitable place could be found however, and thus the idea of a farm was abandoned. Daniel Mahon, the youngest son of our missionary hero, then offered to start the work in Lichtenburg, but it was an exceedingly hard field.

So much diamond stealing and smuggling was going on, and so many apparently honest people had been ensnared into crooked dealings in this connection that the most rigid laws were made. Nobody was allowed to go into the compounds where the natives lived without a permit, and it was

---

[37] Present-day Botswana.
[38] Northern Zimbabwe.

impossible to open a day school in any of the forty-five-odd compounds on the diamond diggings.

Furthermore the work was hampered by the fact that the missionaries had no native workers to help them, and could get very few to attend meetings. Here is a short record of the trip of Dan and his wife to Bechuanaland:

They made for the Genisa Reserve, where there were about six thousand natives. The chief welcomed them gladly, and would have liked them to stay with him, but said they should first ask permission of the resident Magistrate. This gentleman declared he would much appreciate their starting work on the reserve, but that since the first comers there were the London Missionary Society (LMS), their permission must first have to be sought. In other words, there was no freedom of religion there, but the LMS had a monopoly.

Since the LMS headquarters was only a few miles away, Mr and Mrs Dan Mahon went to see the superintendent. He was absent and his place was occupied by a deputy. This gentleman was quite polite until they explained that they would like to commence evangelising on the Genisa Reserve. At

A native hut on the diggings

once he took them to a map, on which almost every reserve in the country was marked by a red dot, an indication that it was under the care of the LMS He told them, "We cannot allow you to enter these reserves, but any others you may evangelise." In other words they would only have been left a very few isolated groups of natives in the wildest and most inaccessible parts of the deserts, where the intense heat would have made it almost impossible for Europeans to live.

The Bechuana as a whole are an intelligent and educated race. Education, industrialism, better agriculture and medicine had done much to ameliorate their physical conditions, but they were still heathen at heart. Moreover, educated and intelligent heathenism is the worst possible form of heathenism.

To return to our story: Dan turned away from Bechuanaland with the sad realisation that the door was closed.

When they had started out on this trip, old Mrs Mahon had said, "My son, if God closes the door in Bechuanaland, do not come back without first visiting Lichtenburg." It was thus that we saw them seeking from the Commissioner of Mines leave to start a mission on the diamond diggings. No other mission was at work there, and a parcel of land was granted them, as well as permission to visit the compounds at any time.

Imagine the situation. They were surrounded by thousands of educated natives. Men who had learned of Christ but had not experienced His power to save. They had been made "children of God" with a few drops of water from a Christening font, but had never experienced the new birth. Furthermore these natives were embittered against the whole white race. Swindled, often denied their wages, exploited and ground down, they were a seething mass of inarticulate discontent and rebellion against everything white.

Here were a few strangers settling among them, and wishing to tell of Christ's power to save. They knew all about that.

What good was it to them? "A few more rascals" they supposed, who had come to exploit them like so many other white men had done. Under these depressing conditions Brother and Sister Dan Mahon and Brother and Sister Fales commenced work in August 1930, preaching in the open air, praying with the sick, and distributing gospel tracts.

We cannot pass this point without referring to the splendid work of the Roodepoort Mission Press. Brothers Mahon and Fales were able to obtain from them sound gospel literature in at least a dozen different languages, and, this literature was given freely, for Christ's sake. God alone knows the glorious results achieved by the Roodepoort Mission Press.

Later, Mr Dan Mahon was transferred to Johannesburg , and Mr and Mrs Fales continued the work alone. He would set out visiting the compounds on his cycle, and the vastness of his parish could be imagined, when it was stated that he evangelised in forty-five different compounds , giving out gospel literature in English, Dutch, Sesotho, Zulu, Xhosa, Pondo, Thembu, Swazi, Hottentot, Sechuana, Sepedi, Shangaan, Kalanga, Venda, Shona, Ndebele and other languages. At times the work was most discouraging.

Two big tent campaigns were held, and over one hundred professed faith in the Lord Jesus, but at the end of two months only four of those could be found who still continued faithful to God and to their confession. Others may have returned to their distant villages, and still remained faithful, and that is just where the trial of the missionaries' faith was most severe. They saw so few per-manent results. God has however, promised that if we cast our bread upon the waters, we shall find it after many days. It was so in the case of these tent campaigns. Some of the seed sprang to life after a lapse of a year or two.

Such was the experience of a Rhodesian Zulu[39] named Dube "zebra". He heard the message, but took his time to think it over, and slowly came to a decision that he must embrace it. After a lapse of many months, he eventually came out boldly for the Lord Jesus, and became a stalwart pillar in the Church. Similarly, from time to time, the missionaries found out that on distant farms there were Christians who had come to the Lord Jesus on the diggings.

The missionaries suffered two tremendous handicaps in their encouragement of the natives to live holy lives:

The Sechuana Bible had been translated by two societies that do not set their faces against beer-drinking, and very much is made of the fact that, according to the Sotho Bible, Christ turned water into beer. There was a malt factory at Germiston, and the natives somehow managed to get hold of the malt. With this they could readily prepare their alcohol, and drunkenness was almost universal.

Furthermore, when a man wished to buy a wife, his relatives assisted him. Later, however, they would declare that they, too, had a right to that woman. This lead to a condition which approached promiscuity, and was too disgraceful to permit description. So low was the condition of morality that the local Government even issued marriage licences valid for only six months, regarding that as about the limit of time that man and wife could be expected to live together.

We saw how much blessing was brought into the gospel ministry through native choirs. Soon after commencing the Lichtenburg work, Brother Fales formed a choir of the first converts. They certainly learnt to sing splendidly, but he had to disband them. The fact was that while these natives were singing angelically upon the streets and in open-air meetings, at the same time they were living in sin, and going

---

[39] Many Zulus had fled from Tshaka as far as Southern Rhodesia (modern Zimbabwe).

back to the drunkenness and adultery that they had professed to have left.

Now the Lichtenburg missionaries were having much better success for they had formed a choir of the best voices among their Sunday scholars, and felt that these young lives, consecrated to God in early years, were a far better testimony to His glory and the saving power of Christ. The Sunday school work was one of the brightest features of the Lichtenburg testimony. So keen were the children that they would have liked to have Sunday school seven days a week.

God had certainly confirmed the preaching of the Word by the most miraculous signs following. There were amazing cases where the sick and suffering had been raised from death's door. Yet, even here, it was very grieving to see such people went right back into heathenism as soon as they had been relieved of their diseases. The missionaries' faith was sorely tried. At times they were tempted to wonder if it was worthwhile. But then God graciously gave them some glorious trophies of His saving power, and at the same time fresh courage to go forward.

The conversion of John Moloi was an instance of this. He had been a witchdoctor, deceiving the people and being deceived himself. He fell ill and could do nothing to cure himself. Then his little daughter was saved at the Sunday school, and brought the precious message home to her parents. God used this to soften their hearts and they brought their charms to be destroyed, and turned in faith to the Lord Jesus.

One cannot leave the record of Lichtenburg Mission without speaking of the printing press. Brother and Sister Fales not only used abundance of literature produced by other presses, but established an efficient printing plant of their own where they turned out thousands of tracts for free distribution, as well as doing most creditably the routine printing of the whole Mission.

Chapter 14

Germiston Assembly

Germiston Location[40], a place where the natives lived, was known among them as "Dukathole" (the wandering calf). The reason for this name was this: when boys and girls wandered from home, their parents knew that the first place to look for them would be in the Germiston Location, but that the children would henceforth not be amenable to any home influence. They would be like wandering cattle.

There were some fourteen thousand natives and a few Asians in this location. They were supposed to consist solely of those who were employed by white people in the town. In reality, however, the law was constantly evaded. The compound often accommodated prostitutes, "skokiaan queens," who thrived by illicit trade in native beer, and other shifty characters.

Into this compound came a Christian family, Mr and Mrs Hadebe, with their three daughters. They were simple black folk like the rest of the people there, but their hearts ached at the wickedness around them. They were determined not only to keep their own souls clean but to witness to others of God's power to save people from sin. They rented just one room. It had to be divided into two for the accommodation

---

[40] Close to Johannesburg.

of their little family, so a big curtain was hung down the centre, and here the five children of God lived, while the long row of rooms on each side of them was so given up to evil that their hearts ached. They started services on Sundays, Wednesdays and Fridays. At first nobody would come. After much persuasion, two of Mrs Hadebe's cousins came to Christ.

Meanwhile, Grace Hadebe was busily studying at school. She was only a little slip of a girl but she had a big heart. In that heart was a mighty determination that one day she would start a school for the children that swarmed in the location, drinking in its sin from their earliest years.

At last she passed her sixth grade and began to teach her sisters. Then the neighbours' children commenced to attend. The crowd grew until they came by dozens, each with a sixpence[41] a month to cover expenses. Even when some conveniently forgot their sixpence, she continued to teach them.

When numbers reached a hundred, her father rented another room and helped her by taking the responsibility for some of her pupils. Then an appeal was sent to Mooigelegen. Money was forwarded with which they purchased an old wood and iron building, and a third teacher was sent to help. The work continued to grow. A Miss Buch and later Miss Johnson went to help with the higher classes and to evangelise the area. The old wood and iron building now did service as a church, while other rooms were rented for some of the classes.

Grace Hadebe displayed a delightful humility throughout, ever ready to help in any form of the school or church work. Because of her love and patience, little children clung to her. She prayed even the most unruly and mischievous into blessing and salvation.

---

[41] A six penny coin – 45 US cents.

In 1930 a new location was built. It adjoined the old one and a simple brick church and school building was erected to accommodate the still growing work.

Meanwhile, Grace Hadebe was slowly dying. She refused to give way to her illness. She would even call the children to her chair to be taught. In the early days of her testimony, she suffered much persecution from the neighbours. At times when she was not able to preach she would sing the gospel, and this led to Grace and her father composing a number of gospel hymns and choruses in Zulu. Gradually the bitterness gave way to respect and admiration. When they realized little Grace was dying, they seemed to awaken to her sterling worth. In June of 1930 she was carried into the new church for the opening services and looked around upon the answer to her prayers. Over two hundred children in simple, neat uniforms, Christian members of the assembly, and a number of European and native visitors were there.

A few days later, after sending a farewell message to her beloved Missionary and announcing that she was going to a big meeting , she asked for her Bible and clasping it to her breast, she fell asleep in her Lord Jesus. Grace Hadebe was only twenty-four when she died, but what a glorious testimony she left! Such works as these were after Mahon's own heart. He would not waste his time by going after those groups where there was no one to carry on the testimony, but preferred to go to hold tent meetings and evangelistic services where he could leave responsible believers to carry on the work after the souls were won and the campaign over. He would emphasize again and again: "This is not my work; it is the Lord's. You are not responsible to me but to Him. It is God Himself who will in due time reward you for what you do in His name".

If we were asked in what one thing Mr Mahon especially excelled, we would say, "In his love and understanding of his fellow man." He was equally at home, equally courteous, whether he was addressing a high government official, a powerful native chief, or a wee black herd boy.

Even in the most delicate affairs of native church life, he would encourage the natives to act upon their own initiative under the guidance of the Holy Spirit. If he gave advice he made it appear as if the guidance came from their own hearts, and so the black folk learned to trust God and not merely their white leader. He knew well enough that if he were to offer a wage to the natives who pastored the many assemblies under his care, they would have always looked to him and would always have been dependent on the white man and the work would be regarded in native eyes as a 'white man's work', and all the pastors and preachers would be white man's employees.

Grace Hadebe, like hundreds of others, was given fullest scope for her own development. She was made to feel, "They are looking to me. They rely upon me. God has put this work into my hands." This drew from her the very best that was in her brave little heart.

Chapter 15

Startling Reactions

If the honest and disinterested learned to admire these messengers of the Cross, the lifeless professors of religion became more and more incensed against them. Thus, it came about that during the rebellion that occurred in 1914, Mr Mahon was awakened in the dead of night, and told, "You must get away without a moment's delay. They are already plotting to kill you." He crept into hiding, and after making due preparation for the carrying on of the farm, he made for Natal.

A very lean time followed, for though he had escaped death by the bullet, he was facing a lingering death by starvation, and had absolutely no resources or means of support. At last he determined to return home in disguise with native companions. They travelled at night and hid in thickets and riverbeds during the day.

One very early dawn they were surprised to see horsemen approaching and almost upon them. Mahon said, "Throw yourselves on your faces and pray." The riders passed within a few feet of them without seeing them. On another occasion a native called "Shh! Quiet! I hear horses' feet." They slipped into a stream, crouching down against the bank until only their heads were above water. In perfect silence they listened for the approaching horsemen, but the sounds became no louder nor softer. Then a native broke into a hearty laugh, saying, "It's that old bull-frog making his noise." And so it was, but it sounded so exactly like horses' hoofs at a distance that it cost the whole party a good wetting.

At last they reached home. Mr Mahon dared not allow it to be known that he was there, so he disguised himself as a Mosotho, putting a coloured blanket about him, and wearing a broad-brimmed Basuto hat that cast a shade over his white face. Thus arrayed he moved about his farm, attending to his crops, until the rebellion was crushed and safety restored.

At another time the work was suffering keenly from a wrong spirit, which had crept in among some of the Christians. Nobody can deny that these black folk had real cause for complaint. Unjust and partial legislation had put them at a disadvantage. The colour bar disqualified them for certain trades and positions which they could hold as well as a white man.

The poor natives tried to adjust their ills with carnal weapons. Political agitation, communism and tradesunionism became potent forces in their minds for righting their many wrongs, that many natives made these a kind of religion. They preached and dreamed of "driving the white man into the sea," of "throwing off the European yoke," and a lot more. This was not the place to discuss the rights or wrongs of such movements and sentiments. At least every Christian would agree that it was fatally wrong to abandon faith in the Lord Jesus Christ for the sake of propagating a political creed.

The missionaries showed the utmost longsuffering with the agitators. Had these black folk realised it, they were turning against their best friends when they endeavoured to foment discord in the churches, and to arouse the natives against their white teachers. The whole Church suffered. How could an assembly be at its best for God when it was divided? It was when "they were with one accord in one place" that the fire of God fell in the Early Church, and discord is one of Satan's most successful weapons.

How many anxious days and sleepless nights these agitations caused the missionaries! Eventually however, the break came. Paul says that divisions are a necessity that those who are approved may be manifest. It proved thus in the Mahon Mission. It was a sieve that let out the undesirables, and kept in those who were on fire for God. For a time the white folk were cut to the heart to see their best-loved native friends leave them in a spirit of violence and hatred. Soon however, the tables turned. One by one the genuine ones crept back, with many sighs of contrition and many expressions of regret. It was good for them that they had tasted the pigs' husks in the far country, that they had felt the pangs of spiritual hunger. They had taken for granted the heroic self-sacrifices of their white leaders. Now they realised how much these blessings cost. Never before did the meetings seem so sweet or fellowship with God's children so precious. The prodigals had strayed, but all who were truly sons had come back to their Father's house and were satisfied at His table.

The brewing of beer was a difficulty that faced the natives as soon as they became Christians. However, Mr Mahon and his fellow workers from the very first set their faces against it. They would have no half-measures. This brought them into unwilling conflict with certain other missions who closed their eyes to beer-drinks and even to drunkenness. One woman came home saved and told her husband, "I will obey you in every good thing, but please do not ask me to brew beer." He was furious. He tried threatening, arguing, persuading, but all to no purpose. At last he took a sjambok[42] of hippopotamus hide and gave her an awful thrashing. He was accustomed to his wives shrieking and cursing under such treatment. This woman said meekly, "You may hit me

---

[42] Similar to a bullwhip, but much shorter.

harder if you like. You can only hurt the body; the spirit is safe in Jesus' keeping." The husband was so amazed that he repented and is now a bright believer.

Another man was so enraged with his Christian wife who refused to brew beer that he threatened her with death. He even took his assegai (spear) and began to sharpen it ominously. She thought that this was mere intimidation until he flung her down, knelt upon her body, and thrust the assegai into her chest, attempting to reach her heart. She seized the weapon and called for help. Relatives ran to her aid and pulled the man off. He was promptly arrested and given a long term in prison. The woman's condition was critical. Her lungs were pierced and frothy blood came from the wound as well as her mouth. However, believers gathered around her and prayed. God graciously spared her life. The wound healed slowly. Finally she was able to go to visit her husband in prison. She would take him little dainties of food. Her kindness after his awful brutality so melted his heart that he was converted. As soon as he came out of prison, he joined the fellowship of the saints and became a local preacher.

When Mr Bryant left South Africa, his native work in Johannesburg was put into the hands of a certain Shabalala, and later was cared for by a Basotho, Walter Ndebele. The assembly was too big for him, however. He carried it on for years, but became involved in political issues and anti-European activities. The numbers went down, for those who were really spiritual would not mix themselves with such propaganda.

 At last Mr Mahon's youngest son Daniel, with his wife and children, left Lichtenburg, and took charge of the Johannesburg Church. He had received his Bible training at the Moody Bible Institute in Chicago, and had been working for God from the age of sixteen. God blessed his efforts. Soon the Church was afire with zeal for God. Thousands of souls flocked to the gold mines from all parts of Africa. The precious message of salvation spread away into distant parts of the country where white missionaries never went. Even in Portuguese East Africa they heard of numbers who had turned to Christ among the Shangaans. They were not able to go and visit these groups of believers, but news came through from time to time, of more souls added to the Lord and of saints walking in the joy and fear of God.

116

Chapter 16

His Last
Earthly Camp Meeting

For weeks beforehand, the notices of the Annual Christmas Meetings had gone out into the hot lowlands of Natal and the wild mountains of Basutoland. The word had passed from one group to another in the great labour compounds of the gold mines along the Witwatersrand and sent to the saints at work in the gravel pits of the diamond fields.

Expectations rose high. One group met another at the various railway sidings or along the dusty roads of the Orange Free State. The slow oxen drew the great lumbering wagons full of singing women and children, while the elder children and the men walked or rode on horseback. Even old women put together their bundles of food and clothing and set out to tramp barefooted five long days over rocky, mountainous country to give their testimony at Etembeni. As they recognised fellow Christians from other villages, they stopped to greet them. Then they would kneel together in prayer, asking God's blessing on the meetings and so continued along the sun-drenched roads.

At night, as they camped together around the glowing bonfires, they practised the hymns and songs they were to sing in the choir and spoke in happy terms of the blessing they had received at other camp meetings. They talked of the great gatherings in the hills, of riverbank crowds as they had gone down into the waters of baptism, and of the triumphs over every difficulty in the name of the Lord Jesus. Sickness was no reason for staying away. Rather it was an incentive to go, for many had gone to camp meetings sick and had gone away gloriously healed.

(Not every camp meeting was held at Mooigelegen, for it was planned to give each corner of the field a due consideration.)

That Christmas however, the dear old father, who had spent his life in the work, was nearing the end of his earthly journey. Naturally, he desired to be at that, his last, camp meeting. As we write he is enjoying the sweet fellowship of the saints in glory. He is "with Christ, which is very far better."

Everyone spoke with such tenderness and respect of "die Ou Baas[43]", Moruti[44], Elder Mahon, Baba[45], Mfundisi[46] and several other names. He was called Reverend, Mynheer[47], Dominee[48] and many more, but it was not the title as much as it was the affection behind it which was so touching.

Young giants from the neighbouring farms rode over at intervals to ask, "How goes it with the old gentleman?" Their fine sun-bronzed faces showed a genuine sympathy as they heard of restless days and sleepless nights. Mrs Mahon was worn out with patient nursing, and had come very near to a breakdown. Thus it was a most gracious provision that Miss Tilley Burkey, a trained nurse and a member of the

---

[43] Afrikaans for "the old master".
[44] Sesotho for "pastor".
[45] "Father in Zulu.
[46] "Teacher" in Zulu.
[47] "Sir" in Dutch.
[48] "Minister" in Dutch and Afrikaans.

Mission, was able to undertake much of the nursing, while sons and sons-in-law helped with night duty. In little groups of two and three, the native ministers who had served for so many faithful years side by side with Mr Mahon, came quietly in to greet him and pray with him.

Two motor trucks started to ply between the station and the Mission Farm, a distance of fifteen miles, bringing in the natives who had come by train. On the farm itself all was quiet, methodical activity. While the ladies were putting up curtains and attending to household linen and bedding, the men were repairing another motor truck and erecting the two big tents in such a way that they would form one vast meeting place. Here firewood was being cut up. Yonder two great oxen and five sheep were being portioned out. One thousand five hundred pounds of corn meal was rationed to the visitors.

The younger generation did all they could to relieve the mind of their father, but he could not rest until assured that such-and-such portions of meat had been given to the believers from Germiston, and that those from Thabong had been accorded due provision. He had planned these

Cooking in a corner of the camp

gatherings so often that to the end he had his fingers upon the pulse of the whole arrangement.

Presently the great wagons came lumbering over the horizon. What shouts of "Khotso," "Ukutula", and similar equivalents for "Peace be unto you!" What shaking of hands and happy greetings! More wagons and still more! Late into the night the motor trucks were bringing their loads of believers. Then guttural cries were heard down at the river. A wagon was stuck, and not all the urging of the oxen could pull it through. Lanterns twinkled in the darkness. A score of ready hands helped. The great creaking "ship of the veld" came slowly up the hill and was brought to rest on the camping ground.

In the early hours of the morning it sounded as though the heavens had come down to earth. Singing, and, oh, what singing! These hundreds of black folk were at their morning worship, and the richness of their wonderful voices was like an angelic choir.

A visit to the camp showed a long line of carts and wagons near which the women were already bending over their cooking pots. Their babies were strapped on their backs in blankets and the whole was wreathed in coils of smoke from the open fires.

It was Christmas morning and by ten o'clock the white farmers began to arrive. Some had come long distances by car and Cape-cart. Now occurred one of the most touching incidences of the whole gathering. In spite of his weakness, Mr Mahon wanted to be at the midday service. He could not even lift a hand to feed himself, but at least he could lift his voice in a last appeal to the black people whom he loved, to trust in the Lord Jesus who had lived and died for them, and to the believers to live for Christ alone.

The poor limbs that had tramped so many thousand miles were now useless. How was he to get to the tent? In touching sympathy those splendid young Dutchmen had arranged it all. Years before, they had been deceived. They had been told as children not to offer their hands in greeting to the Mahons because the Mahons worked among the Natives[49]. Today a pole was fixed each side of the "Old Warrior's" chair and these neighbouring farmers lifted it tenderly, almost reverently, and carried it four-a-side. When the first eight were tired, another eight and another were there to take a turn, until Mr Mahon was seated in the midst of his beloved converts.

His voice was not strong, but word for word his oldest son repeated the message so that all in the tent might hear it. Ministers and elders of other denominations also took part. There were scores of white folk and about a thousand natives present. The messages were interpreted into Zulu, Sesotho and English. There were choir pieces, solos, and most wonderful testimonies.

For two days the services continued, but the man whose faith and courage had been the human instrument in bringing these multitudes to Jesus' feet was carried gently home and did not leave the house again until his body was laid to rest on the 10th of January, 1936, and his brave spirit returned to God who gave it.

---

[49] The first edition of the book used the derogatory term the farmers would have used.

Postscript

We have endeavoured to tell something of God's dealings with a man, and of the blessings which followed that man as the Holy Spirit matured and directed him. Very naturally this has led to our telling something of his family, his fellow-workers, and the vast work which, under God's directions, he brought into being. We have been tempted strongly to tell more of the blessed ministry of those other splendid members of Mr Mahon's band. This, however, would call for many more volumes. Thus we can only say that, although God has called home his tired worker, the glorious testimony which he and his dear wife established, still went forward in blessing and power.

Mrs Mahon and her sons and daughters who continued the work. Alfred is front left, Dan front right and Evaline is standing second from the right

123

124

Printed in Poland
by Amazon Fulfillment
Poland Sp. z o.o., Wrocław